New Discoveries in Afterlife Communication

Proceedings of the 38th Annual Conference of the
Academy for Spiritual and Consciousness Studies

Editor
R. Craig Hogan, Ph.D.

i

The Authors in This Book

The authors in this book are the presenters at the New Developments in Afterlife Communication conference held by the Academy for Spiritual and Consciousness Studies in Scottsdale, Arizona, July 11-13, 2014. For information about the conference, DVD or audio recordings, or the Academy for Spiritual and Consciousness Studies, go to the Academy website:

http://ascsi.org

ASCS Publications contact:
      Academy for Spiritual and Consciousness Studies
      P.O. Box 84
      Loxahatchee, Florida 33470

ISBN 978-0-9802111-9-1

ASCS Publications

Contents

Death ends a life, not a relationship.

- Jack Lemon

Preface

Until this century, while some people experienced personal spontaneous afterlife contacts in dream visitations, physical signs, and fleeting glimpses of loved ones, people could not easily communicate with their loved ones in the afterlife at will. Those who wanted to communicate with loved ones in the afterlife had to seek out a medium for a reading. For ordinary people on the Earth plane, the next realm of life we call the afterlife was inaccessible and frightening.

However, that condition is changing, dramatically and rapidly. Today, ordinary people with no medium abilities are learning how to communicate with their loved ones in spirit. New methods of communicating that require no medium abilities are being discovered, refined, and taught to grieving people. Today, virtually anyone can have a direct, unmediated afterlife communication with loved ones in the afterlife.

There is such an array of these methods of afterlife communication that the Academy for Spiritual and Consciousness Studies devoted its 38th annual conference to having 21 researchers, developers, and practitioners describe to attendees the new methods of afterlife communication they have originated, are using, or are teaching. This book is a compilation of papers written by the presenters, containing the same information provided at the conference. They are the conference proceedings.

Contacts with Other Levels of Consciousness via Devices, and Scientific Evidence

Sonia Rinaldi, M.S.

(Sonia's first of two sessions at the conference)

Abstract

The paper presents transimages of deceased apparitions or transfigurations recorded via electronic devices. It includes a number of cases in which voice and images were captured, including some American cases recorded specifically for the New Developments in Afterlife Communication conference. The paper explains the biometric analyses showing measurements of the images proportions and providing analyses of the images.

Contacts with Other Levels of Consciousness via Devices, and Scientific Evidence

by Sonia Rinaldi

The communication with the Other Side via electronic equipment is what we call instrumental transcommunication (ITC).

We can record either images, or more precisely, videos, and voices. I know that usually when we talk about ITC, people associate it with voices or whispers that are difficult to hear and understand. However, ITC is much more than that. The speakers from the afterlife can speak as clear as we do, and the images can be extremely clear.

In this paper, I focus specifically on the transimages because as a phenomenon, the images are more important than the audio of voices. Why? Because they are universal and because they require a much higher level of technology. What that means is that their science is superior to ours. The knowledge these friends have is amazing to say the least.

In the area of transimages, we have many, many different phenomena, but in this paper I will explain deceased apparitions. I have decided to include scientific evidence, so I will show some biometric analyses of the images.

Objectives

In Sao Paulo, Brazil, I coordinate the Institute of Advanced Research in Instrumental Transcommunication. We have two objectives:

1. To support people in grief

2. To authenticate ITC phenomena that provide evidence of survival after death, and the reality of interdimensional communication evaluated using scientific parameters

This is the task of a group that I created inside the institute, which I call the pool of investigators. It is composed only of engineers, physicists, and computer scientists.

They study all phenomena happening in my lab, trace the lines of possible theories to explain what is happening, and develop all manner of analyses.

Transfiguration

Because transfiguration will be the basis of my paper, it is important for you to know what it is. Transfiguration is the metamorphic power ascribed to certain mediums to assume facial characteristics of deceased people.

> It was as though the medium's face were of plastic material being rapidly molded from one form to another: oriental faces, Indians, calm, dignified, serious, spiritual, in short, almost every type of face was depicted during the most unusual séance. (William J. Erwood, *The National Spiritualist*, 1931).

We can add the description of transfiguration written by our friend Victor Zammit, also a presenter at this conference, extracted from his book:

> Often many different faces will come one after another—sometimes only seconds apart. Many people recognize the face of a loved one during the display. Below on the left is a transfiguration medium Jean Skinner as she normally is. On the right is a spirit face transfigured over hers.

Today, very few sensitives have such a capacity as we see in Gordon Garforth. In the image to the right, you can see his face in transformation.

Deceased Apparitions or Transfigurations Via Devices

What is explained here is a "hi-tech" version of an old type of mediumship. That is, we can obtain a great number of faces in each recording. The difference between the mediumistic version and the technologic version is that now we can document in a computer and submit it to all sorts of mathematics analysis.

The Phenomenon

1. It occurs in real time—that is, images which are being recorded can be already seen in the PC screen.

2. It happens in extreme velocity. How is that? Let's remember that each second of video has 30 frames. Many times, the transimage is just one frame. So the time they have to create and "print" in our space-time will be one divided by 30. That is very fast.

3. As for what we observe, the action of our spirit friends, or senders as I prefer to call them, is precisely the manipulation of light. Our science is still very far from being able to do this.

Capture Schematics 1

In this image is one of the many processes I use to record pictures of the deceased. I use a transparent plate, plastic, or any shining cloth in front of a person. Usually a relative, parent, or friend of the deceased has come to the lab with the picture we want to register.

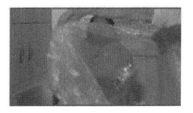

Alin's Case

Below are four Brazilian cases and four American ones. The first is Alin. She lost her son André at the age of 23 in a car accident. She came to my lab and I put her in front of the camera. Many deceased persons appeared, including her son, father, and others. I selected some to show here. Below is the apparition of her mother. Alin's picture is to the right.

Alin´s nose, mouth, and other facial characteristics are very different from her mother´s. Many other relatives appeared as well. Below we see her Aunt Luiza. Notice that for this, I used a bubble plastic in front of Alin´s face.

She also recognized her son, André.

Many unknown faces appeared also. These are some examples:

Biometry

- Biometry is based in the idea that some physical traces are exclusive to each human being.

- The analysis starts by comparing the measurement of the distance between the eyes of the REFERENCE IMAGE.

- After all measurements done, the same will be done to the OBJECT IMAGE.

- The closer the measurements come to 100%, the more similar the faces will be.

Evidence of the Phenomenon

To illustrate the phenomenon, I have chosen the following two images for comparison.

The images were sent to Eng. Paulo Krokinsky, whose doctorate was in biometrics. The first thing he did was to convert both images to black and white. The one on the left is the REFERENCE IMAGE and the one on the right is the OBJECT IMAGE.

The first measurement he took was between the eyes of the REFERENCE IMAGE. Then he took all the other measurements. After that, he did the same for the other image. Here is the table of results:

Table 1: Measurement of Image Reference

		Normalized Values	Comparison	Difference%
Distance between the eyes	77	1		
Eyes level based on the upper jaw	54	0,701298701	1,00382	-0,38197097
Eyes level based on the lower jaw	78	1,012987013	0,912939	8,706108706
lips width	63	0,818181818	0,979136	2,086438152
Height of the lips	16	0,207792208	0,722325	27,76747062
Average of face width	147	1,909090909	0,904959	9,504132231
Average of the eyebrow length	7,1414	0,092745818	0,874061	12,59393789
Height of the face based on the lower jaw	231	3	0,995455	0,454545455
Forehead height based on the	72	0,935064935	1,176892	-17,6892073

eyebrows				
The average width of forehead	138	1,792207792	0,96912	3,088023088
Length of the nose based on the forehead	101	1,311688312	0,99743	0,257034632

Table 2: Measurement of the Image Analyzed

		Normalized Values
Distance between the eyes	73	1
Eyes level based on the upper jaw	51	0,698630137
Eyes level based on the lower jaw	81	1,109589041
Lips width	61	0,835616438
Height of the lips	21	0,287671233
Average of face width	154	2,109589041
Average of the eyebrow length	7,745967	0,106109137
Height of the face based on the lower jaw	220	3,01369863
Forehead height based on the eyebrows	58	0,794520548
The average width of the forehead	135	1,849315068
Length of the nose based on the forehead	96	1,315068493

Conclusion

In some items, the variation was small as in the height of eyes based on the upper jaw whose difference is -0.3819, and the width of the lips with 2,0864%. But other measures show large variations, which suggests that a new face was formed.

As in previous analysis, when a *high-pass* filter is applied, no image is formed, which means that the image consists of low frequencies.

In this way, we can conclude that the new face, or the transimage, is not the same face because it shows large biometric differences.

High Pass Filter Test

In the original image, the image is formed even with a *high-pass* filter. The image formed using the *high-pass* filter is on the left.

The same does not occur with the image analyzed, which means that the paranormal image has intrinsic characteristics that differ from the original (on the far right).

Explanation

High frequencies show sudden variations forming the image as the outline of a face relative to the bottom of the image.

A certain point of an image or pixel is the representation of light intensity and its representation in time is from left to right, so we would have a t=0 time on the far left and on the far right a t1=X time where X is the amount of time required to represent all the pixels of a line drawn from left to right.

So, if we imagine only one row from left to right, it would be a low-frequency event because it required the entire X time to be represented. Analogously, a point would be the highest frequency to be represented because it requires only one unit of time for its representation. Therefore changes in image points, considering their vicinity, determines their frequency.

High-pass filters show sudden changes and enhances contour details in most applications. Our friends use bubble wrap, veil, or other filter as a *low-pass* filter to create the transimages. They use this resource to modify the images.

Study of Frequencies in Images

The paranormal image to the right occurred over my face. Transforming both images into black and white and applying a bass-pass filter, notice that both become soft. However, applying a high-pass filter, my original image becomes strongly defined while the transimage disappears. This means that the paranormal images are built of low frequencies only.

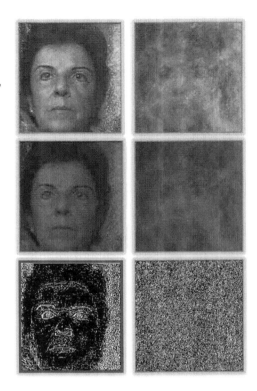

Marlene's Case

We performed this experiment with Dr. Karin, a medical doctor, and her father, Dr. Djalma. Dr. Karin contacted me because she wanted news about her deceased mother, Marlene. In fact, Marlene appeared and was recognized by her daughter and husband. To the right are transimages that we registered while Karin was with us. Her deceased mother's picture is to the right in the first pair.

Biometric Analysis

An analysis was done by Eng. Paulo Krokisnky. Initially, he converted the transimage (top right below) and the reference Image (top left below) into black and white. The black-and-white versions appear in the bottom pair of pictures below.

The analysis of these images follows.

Table 3: Measurement of the Image Reference

	Value (pixels)	Percentage
Distance between the eyes	73	73
Eyes level based on the upper jaw	59	0,80821918
Eyes level based on the lower jaw	150	2,05479452
Lips width	56	0,76712329
Height of the lips	39	0,53424658
Average of face width	160	2,19178082
Average of the eyebrow length	5,66	0,07753425
Height of the face based on the lower jaw	246	3,36986301
Forehead height based on the eyebrows	71	0,97260274
The average width of the forehead	125	1,71232877
Length of the nose based on the forehead	59	0,80821918

Table 4: Measurement of the Image Analyzed

		Normalized Values
Distance between the eyes	73	73
Eyes level based on the upper jaw	91	1,24657534
Eyes level based on the lower jaw	135	1,84931507
Lips width	67	0,91780822
Height of the lips	25	0,34246575
Average of face width	164	2,24657534
Average of the eyebrow length	6,86	0,0939726
Height of the face based on the lower jaw	229	3,1369863
Forehead height based on the eyebrows	59	0,80821918
The average width of the forehead	140	1,91780822
Length of the nose based on the forehead	111	1,52054795

Results

The further the results are from 100, the more different the images are, as shown in Table 5.

Table 5: Percentual Similarity

Percentual similarity
100
154,237288
90
119,642857
64,1025641
102,5
121,201413
93,0894309
83,0985915
112
188,135593

Conclusion

Again the differences between both measurements point out that the transimage is, in fact, another face.

Tatiana's Case

Maria Isabel's daughter, Tati, passed away from bone cancer at the age of 27. A dozen deceased people appeared during the recording session, including Bel, her husband, and son.

To the right and below are some results. Using wrap plastic, an unknown blond teenager appeared.

However, Bel's dream was to have news about

her beloved daughter, Tati. In fact, Tati was one of the many young women that appeared. Below, Bel maintains her traces of a woman of 52 years old. Nevertheless, the young girl is remarkably different:

More than that, Tati appeared as a young lady but also as a child (see the transimage below). Both appeared over Bel's face.

American Cases: Capture Schematics 2 — Transimages via Skype

Craig's Mom Apparition

This was the first experiment via Skype. A friend, Nilza, and I connected our computers so that she was filming my room and I was recording hers. She sat in front of the camera and I filmed her face. Different images appeared over her, including Craig´s mom. Below we see Nilza at left, the transpicture in the middle, and Craig´s mom at right.

Apparitions Over a Photo

As Craig had sent me the photo of his Family, I decided to test something new. To record the photo itself, to see if our Spirit Friends could act over it too.

They did. Over the photo, many changes happened. Below, to the left is Craig when he was a child. In the center, he became an older little girl. In the right picture, his father changed into an old man, with white hair and older features.

 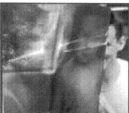 

Some other changes happened over Craig´s father. One detail is particularly important. In the photo, Craig´s father's head is rotated a bit to the right side, but in the transimage, he appears looking to the camera. Surprisingly, a lady appears, also looking toward the camera.

Natalie Johnson (deceased in December 2009)

Thanks to Craig, I could record and get amazing transimages of four American kids. Let me tell you about the first case.

This beautiful little girl is Natalie. She lived in Loda, Illinois, and was a perfectly healthy child. She loved to play with her little sister and friends, took piano lessons, and participated in the school band and chorus.

She competed in gymnastics competitions on the trampoline and in tumbling. She loved babies and children so much that she wished to become a teacher to spend time with kids.

At the age of 11, one Saturday she suddenly felt bad and had a low grade fever. On Sunday, the fever was gone, but she had a stomach ache and felt nauseous. On Monday, she was taken to the family doctor who said it was a stomach virus and prescribed antinausea medication.

That day, Natalie and her mother made plans to watch a movie together on Tuesday. But Tuesday morning she had a seizure, fell into a coma, and was transported to the hospital via ambulance. The doctors performed many tests, but Natalie never awoke.

After her passing, the illness was diagnosed as sepsis, most likely mengiococcemia (bacteria in the blood).

We can all imagine the suffering of this family with such an unexpected tragedy.

To the right is the schematics used for capturing in this case. I recorded her picture from a notebook screen.

Below are two family pictures. The first is Natalie with her cat, Snowball. The second is a picture of her dog Sammie. It seems that both appeared in the recordings.

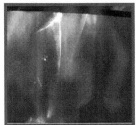

This transimage may represent snowball.

This transimage may represent Sammie

In the lower left picture, notice that Natalie´s picture is directly behind the film and a cat appears in the lower left, in front. In addition, Natalie seems to be blinking.

Another very special fact was that a "doll" appeared over Natalie´s photo as you can see below. It may be a reference to the doll Rebeca, an American girl brand doll that Natalie wanted for Christmas that year, that was placed in her coffin at the visitation. Notice that the transimage (doll) looks in a different direction compared with Natalie´s photo behind. Other dolls appeared in Natalie´s place.

Among the pictures kindly sent by Natalie's mother, Stephanie, there was this one of Debbie's family in which an old doll was possibly a present for one of the girls. It is similar to the old doll that appeared in the recordings. The image of the doll follows.

In Natalie's place in the photo many faces appeared; one of them was Briggitte, this lady:

 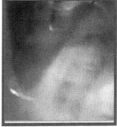

Natalie's Cousin's Apparition

Surprisingly, the apparition of a brunette girl appeared, replacing Natalie's picture in the recording. The question was: WHO could that girl be?

I sent the transimage to Natalie's mother, Stephanie to see if by any chance she knew the deceased girl. She replied positively, telling me that possibly she could be Natalie's deceased cousin. The cousin's mother asked to see the picture. When she saw it, she agreed that it seemed like the image of a brunette girl was her daughter Debbie, who passed at the age of 8 in Columbus, Ohio. As expected, she could be a teenager in the Other Side, precisely as she looks now in the transpicture.

In the picture to the right, Natalie's cousin, Debbie, is in the middle. Below are the picture of Natalie, the transpicture of the brunette girl, and a close-up of Debbie.

Sean and Kyle's Case

Kyle and Sean died after a tragic event.

These kids are Maria Pe´s sons: Sean Robert Fuchs (15) and Kyle Joseph Fuchs (13).

Wonderful boys, happy, healthy. Sean was finishing his first year in high school as a freshman and Kyle had just completed 7th grade. Sean was an accomplished musician and guitar player, and Kyle was an accomplished football player. They had dreams to continue these passions as they grew into adulthood.

Their own father killed both of them by first giving them sleeping pills, then shooting them as they slept in their beds, then the father turned the gun on himself (June - 2011, in San Diego - California).

Recording with Kyle's Photo

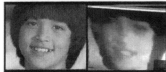

We are already very used to register transfigurations either over a person live in the Lab or over a photo. Though, for the first time we registered with such clearness the alteration our a photo that suggests a trip in time.

It is as if our Spirit Friends wanted to show us how Kyle had grown on the other side and instead of being a child, now he is a teenager. At least this is an amazing demonstration of power over Time, what may be a reference to the possible existence of the Akashic Records.

The same phenomenon seemed to occur with his brother Sean. The sequence of transimages start with the photo and change until the image appears as a young man who is no longer a teenager.

The sequence of Sean's images follows.

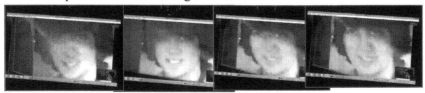

Mickey Morgan's Case

Mickey died at the age of 20 in the mountains of Colorado in 2007. Recording his photo, many deceased persons appeared, such as these two:

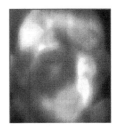

However, I chose this transimage to compare with Mickey´s face and show the evidence of the difference:

Analysis of the Transimage

GREEN makes a better contribution to a clean face perception and analysis.

The inclination of 5 grades of the paranormal image in relation to the photo is significant.

Also a contour of both faces was done and then compared. As we can see Mickey´s face is very different in format as well in the eyes.

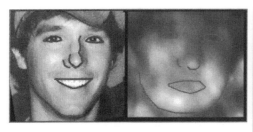

And a last comparison made in Autocad shows images completely different, pointing out that in fact another person appeared.

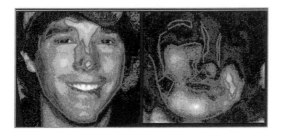

Last Words

Transfiguration is one among many other phenomena in ITC that can equally be studied and investigated by science. I particularly trust that only science may bring the undeniable certainty that Mankind needs to confirm the reality of survival.

My team and I are doing our best to contribute to this.

Biography

Brazilian researcher Sonia Rinaldi has a Mastership Degree in Sciences of Religion. She is an author and lecturer, and is internationally recognized as one of the foremost researchers of instrumental transcommunications (ITC).

Sonia started researching ITC in 1988. She twice received the international Hedri Prize from the Swiss Foundation for Parapsychology for innovative research in 1995 and 1997.

In 2000, Sonia took the research to a scientific lab working with engineers, physicists, and scientists. The result of her studies of instrumental transcommunication has been the ability to record voices from people in spirit using a telephone, with incredible voice quality. She also has developed new techniques to record transimages, which are images that appear when an opaque film is waved over a person's face or some other background.

Bibliography

Zammit, V. (n.d.). "Transfiguration Mediumship." From
http://www.victorzammit.com/evidence/transfiguration.htm.

Seeing and Speaking to the Dead and Other Interdimensional Contacts Via Devices

Sonia Rinaldi, M.S.

(Sonia's second of two sessions at the conference)

Abstract

The paper presents eight transcripts of afterlife voice contacts recorded via a PC. It then describes the types of media that are the means of interdimensional image formation: using over-wrap plastic, photos, images on TV screens, writing on the TV screen, images on metallic paper, created over nature, humanoid apparitions, over plastic plaque, 3D, over a hugs blanket, on walls, and animal apparitions in infrared images. It ends with a summary list of what ITC offers.

Seeing and Speaking to the Dead and Other Interdimensional Contacts via Devices

by Sonia Rinaldi

VOICE CONTACTS

The possibilities in voices research are

1. Recordings with deceased ones
2. Recordings with live persons (coma, Alzheimer's, autistic, multiple sclerosis, brain damaged, and so on)

Devices Used

- Notebook or desktop
- Telephone
- Skype
- Microphone

It is also possible to use a TV, Lauder speaker, and other devices in the audible sound and ultrasound range.

Below are some examples of audios in English.

Example 1

During an experiment of audio and video simultaneously the following audio was recorded and three transimages appeared (of Tatiana, Kaius, and Roberto).

Audio recorded—(female voice): -"I want the photos to arrive!"

Below are the transimages received that day, when that audio was recorded

Transimage 1: Tatiana's apparition over Janaina's photo.

The transimage film was moved over the photo of a woman named Janaina (to the left below). The transimage that resulted is in the center. It is the likeness of a woman in spirit named Tatiana, whose photo is the third photo, to the right.

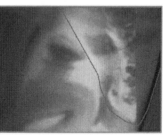

Transimage 2: Kaius' apparition using Stefano's photo.

The second transimage of the apparition of a man named Kaius appeared when the transimage film was manipulated over a photograph of a man named Stefano.

Below, Stafano's photo is to the left, with the film over it. The transimage apparition is in the middle. A photograph of the man in spirit, Kaius, is to the right.

Transimage 3: Roberto's apparition.

Example 2

I asked if any child, or especially Natalie, the young girl who passed from sepsis, would like to leave a message for her mother. In response, a child's voice replies:

Child's voice: "Mommy, I can talk!"

Example 3

I asked my friend Craig's mother if she could say something to her son and a female voice replied

Woman's voice: "Ready at this point!"

Coherent message—his mother is informing her son that the spiritual team is ready to work in ITC with him.

Example 4

As I had found great difficulty in getting replies in English, I wondered whether contact with spirits from the USA is possible. So I asked: "Does it make any sense to you that the deceased cannot come and go freely over the country?"

A male voice says: "Yes I guess!"

I asked if Spirits could not come and go everywhere. This suggests a possible "organization" in the other side.

For instance, could anyone from Saudi Arabia come and inspire terrorism in America?

Possibly, there exist "spiritual" frontiers over the countries. Apparently the entrance is not free everywhere.

Example 5:

I went on, asking about the same theme: "Here on Earth we need a visa to enter a country. Is there something similar in your space?"

The reply confirms my thoughts: "That is right!"

Example 6:

I addressed a question to Craig's father: "Mr. Hogan, what can you tell about the life in spirit? Is it good?"

Reply—"Yes, the best one!"

Example 7:

Usually I also make technical questions. I asked, "Is this sound OK for you?"

Male voice: "I just hope that hears the Planet Alpha there…!"

I asked them if they were speaking from Alpha and a female voice confirmed:

Female voice: "Oh yeaaaah!"

Alpha is frequently mentioned as the place where speakers live. We have around a hundred recordings in which the name Alpha is referred to. Possibly, it is where the transmission station is placed.

Example 8:

Frequently, I change the way of recording or change equipment, always endeavoring to improve the communication. In this example, I was testing the use of an ultrasound sound source that is not exactly ultrasound, but almost. I was using the range of 17.000Kz. Real ultrasound is up to 20.000Hz.

In this case, a male voice replied before my question:

Male voice: "Happy you have contacted me!"

And then I asked: "Can you listen to me?"

A Study of Paranormal Voice

The fundamental frequency (F0) is typically from 85 to 255 Hz. When we record with a microphone, as we must, all human voice has the F0 plus the harmonics. But paranormal voices recorded in the same conditions generally will not have F0.

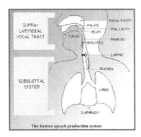

Example

This example is in Portuguese. *"Delícia estar te vendo a sorrir…"* Translation: "Delightful to see you smiling"

Here, the software used by Eng. F. Collier was Audacity 3.0.2 and Praat 5.3. The first thing he did was to separate the vowels, and then he chose one. He chose the "a" from "estar."

The "a" from "estar" is clearly pitch-marked. The yellow arrow on the diagram on the next page points to the place on the screen at which the pitch is marked.

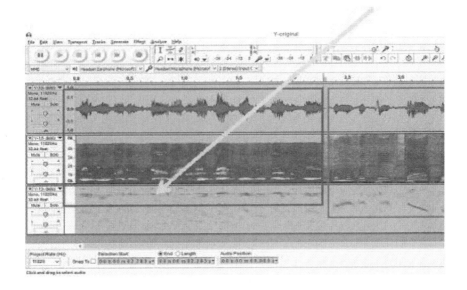

Now we can notice that where a human voice would appear, the paranormal voice doesn´t.

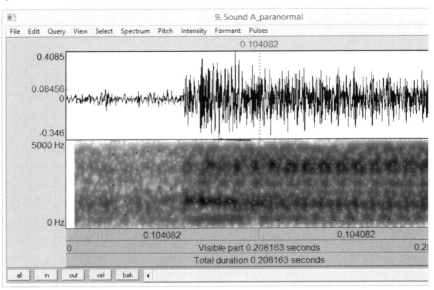

THE MEANS OF INTERDIMENSIONAL CONTACTS VIA DEVICES

A general overview of my work will show that ITC is not simply poorly recorded voices. In truth, ITC has been shown to be an incredible tool for communication with other dimensions, with beings having much higher capacity and incredibly advanced science. For instance, these beings are able to create images in all of the following media:

1. Using Over Wrap Plastic

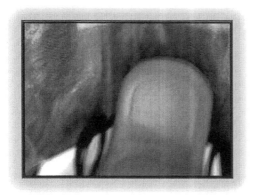

2. In a Photo

The apparition of Jana in spirit appeared in a picture I took with a camera of her mother-in-law, Edna.

3. Images on a TV Screen

4. Writing on the TV Screen

5. Images on Metallic Paper

6. Created Over Nature

7. Humanoid Apparitions

In the following examples, you see my image altered into a humanoid lady and Edna's transfiguration.

8. Over Plastic Plaque

09. 3D

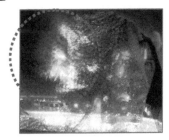

9. Over a Hugs Blanket

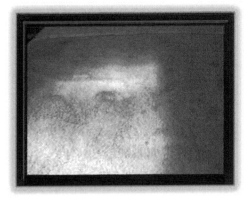

10. On Walls

11. Animal Apparitions in Infrared Images

Conclusion

1. ITC is much more than just whispered voices.

2. ITC seems to offer tools of investigation to science never before available in history.

3. The phenomena's happening in real time makes the possibility of faking difficult.

4. Phenomena leave evidence that communication with higher levels of intelligences has been established.

It is up to us to deserve what these friends may bring to us.

Biography

Brazilian researcher Sonia Rinaldi has a mastership degree in Sciences of Religion. She is an author and lecturer, and is internationally recognized as one of the foremost researchers of Instrumental TransCommunications (ITC).

Sonia started researching ITC in 1988. She twice received the international Hedri Prize from the Swiss Foundation for Parapsychology for innovative research in 1995 and 1997.

In 2000, Sonia took the research to a scientific lab, working with engineers, physicists, and scientists. The result of her studies of instrumental transcommunication has been the ability to record voices from people in spirit using a telephone, with incredible voice quality. She also has developed new techniques to record transimages, which are images that appear when an opaque film is waved over a person's face or some other background.

Self-Guided Afterlife Connections

R. Craig Hogan, Ph.D.

Abstract

The article describes the Self-Guided Afterlife Connection procedure developed by R. Craig Hogan, Ph.D. Craig realized that it is possible for people to connect with loved ones living in the greater reality that is outside of the Earth plane. He had co-authored books with two psychotherapists who were helping people connect with their loved ones using a psychotherapy method called bilateral stimulation. He reasoned that the same state of mind that allowed the afterlife connections could be induced through hypnosis. The Self-Guided Afterlife Connection procedure is a training program that teaches participants how to connect through hypnosis, gradually helping them learn how to take themselves into the connection using self-hypnosis.

The Self-Guided Afterlife Connection procedure is made available freely by the Center for Spiritual Understanding at http://selfguided.spiritualunderstanding.org.

Self-Guided Afterlife Connection

by R. Craig Hogan, Ph.D.

"Oh wow! Oh wow! Oh wow!"

Steve Jobs uttered those words on his deathbed. "Before embarking," his sister wrote, "he'd looked at his sister Patty, then for a long time at his children, then at his life's partner, Laurene, and then over their shoulders past them.

"Steve's final words were: 'Oh wow. Oh wow. Oh wow'"
(Simpson, 2011).

Steve Jobs was still in a physical body, but his vision opened to the underlying realm he was about to become fully part of when the body failed. It wasn't that he was "returning to," "entering," or "crossing over into" an "after" life. The realm he became aware of had been underlying the gaudy physical realm all of his life. Jobs and we voluntarily ignore the underlying realm as we focus our gaze on the physical world to be able to adjust to life's challenges and learn life's lessons.

Thomas Alva Edison, inventor of the light bulb, fell into a coma for a period before his passing. Emerging from the coma for a few moments, Edison looked upwards and said, "It is very beautiful over there" (Beals, 1999). He had lost his focus on the physical realm for a time and was conscious of the underlying reality.

Lawrence and Repede (2013) studied the incidence of deathbed visions in 60 hospice chart audits and 75 survey responses by hospice nurses across the United States. They found that 89% of the hospice nurses reported that patients who experienced a death-bed communication had a peaceful and calm death.

The sensory experiences imposed upon us by the physical realm preoccupy our conscious minds so we're normally unable to experience the underlying reality and connect with people living on the next plane of life. However, the underlying reality comes into awareness and afterlife connections occur naturally and automatically when the body ceases to function. When the body shuts down, the underlying realm that was obscured by our focus on the physical realm fills our consciousness, and loved ones who have transitioned off of the Earth plane become visible and communicate with us.

Since the underlying reality is accessible to all people, it should be possible to enter a state of mind in which a person can become conscious of the people living there, whom we call deceased, and communicate with them.

Until recently, few successful methods had been developed that would allow people to have their own connections with deceased loved ones by accessing the underlying reality. The Monroe Institute's Lifeline was the most successful method during before the turn of the century. Bob Monroe developed an audio aid called Hemi-Sync that brings experiencers into a state of mind in which they are able to interact with people living in the greater reality (Monroe, 1977).

Then, in the last decades of the twentieth century, more methods to help people enter the state of mind in which they could receive messages from people living in the other realms of life were discovered.

Induced After-Death Communications

In 1995, Allan Botkin, Psy.D., a psychotherapist at a Chicago VA hospital, learned how to use eye movement desensitization and reprocessing (EMDR) to help clients have after-death communications during psychotherapy sessions. He named the method Induced After-Death Communication. The use of EMDR brings the client into a state of mind in which the greater reality becomes accessible, and while in the state of consciousness that accesses the greater reality, they communicate with their deceased loved ones. Most clients emphatically state that they have had a real communication with their deceased loved ones, and they view the afterlife differently, even those who started the therapy as atheists. Dr. Botkin and I describe the therapy method and 84 cases in the book, *Induced After-Death Communication: A New Therapy for Grief and Trauma* (2007).

Guided Afterlife Connections

In 2010, Rochelle Wright, M.S., a Washington state-licensed psychotherapist, learned how to use bilateral stimulation to help her clients connect with the people for whom they were grieving. In Guided Afterlife Connections, clients open their own connections with their loved ones in the afterlife, guided by a licensed psychotherapist. The method itself does not induce the connections. The psychotherapist is not a medium and has no influence over the nature or content of the connection. The afterlife connections occur naturally and effortlessly between the experiencers and their loved ones, emerging when the experiencers enter a receptive mode, just as sleep follows naturally from relaxing into a comfortable bed. The connections normally unfold in four to five hours. The procedure is around 95% successful (Wright and Hogan, 2010).

A study with 45 subjects who participated in at least one Guided Afterlife Connections session found that 95% had afterlife connections. Their ratings of the level of disturbance of memories associated with the person who had passed, using the 10-point Subjective Units of Distress (SUDS) scale, showed that disturbance ratings at the beginning of the session averaged 9.42. After one session, the average of ratings had reduced to 1.41, an 85 percent reduction (Hogan, 2012).

The method is described in the book I co-authored with the originator of the method, Rochelle Wright. The book is titled *Guided Afterlife Connections* (2010).

Self-Guided Afterlife Connections

As I co-authored the books about each of these psychotherapy methods, I became convinced that it should be possible to devise a method by which an individual could access the greater reality without a psychotherapist's aid to enter the requisite state of mind. EMDR and bilateral stimulation are too dangerous to teach people to use them on themselves. The procedures break down barriers in the mind that can result in suppressed memories and traumas surfacing. A qualified psychotherapist must be present when those methods are used to help the patient cope with the emerging memories and traumas.

Because I have a background in hypnosis, I reasoned that it should be possible to use hypnosis instead of EMDR or bilateral stimulation to relax the person's preoccupation with the physical realm so the person could connect with loved ones living in the next realm of life we call the afterlife. However, to bring people into the state of mind in which they could allow their minds to connect with loved ones in the afterlife, the person must

- believe the afterlife is a reality

- believe their loved ones are willing to communicate and accessible to communicate

- learn to relax the conscious mind so their minds can allow the underlying reality to become prominent

- learn to allow free unfoldment, in which messages from the person in spirit come into the person's consciousness without control, inhibition, or judgment

- be able to enter a state of mind infused with feelings of love and compassion that seem to enhance the likelihood of an afterlife communication

- be able to enter this state of consciousness at will

- become sensitive to the sense of the loved one's presence

A procedure that satisfied these conditions must be freely accessible to people through the Internet medium so any person anywhere in the world could learn the method.

The pages that follow explain how I developed the Self-Guided Afterlife Connections procedure to satisfy all of these conditions. The procedure is divided into eight stages. Each stage focuses on at least one of these requirements.

Believe the Afterlife is a Reality

Stage 1 explains the importance of having the conviction that the afterlife is a reality. It states that some doubt is natural, but the person who doubts the existence of the afterlife should not go through the procedure hoping that a connection will change that belief.

Skepticism actually inhibits accessing the greater reality. That has been found to be true in what is called the "experimenter effect." An objective researcher in psychic activity may find psychic activity present in experiments while a skeptic performing the same experiment using the same protocols finds no effects that could be attributed to psychic activity (Schlitz, 2014). Skepticism and doubt dampen psychic activity.

The online reading materials explain why conviction that the afterlife is a reality is important to being able to make an afterlife connection. They explain that in our society today, some doubt is natural, but the participants must put the doubt aside and enter into the training with openness and confidence that their loved ones are alive and well, just living in a different place.

This stage ends with a list of resources to learn more about the afterlife.

Believe Their Loved One is Accessible and Willing to Communicate

The Self-Guided Afterlife Connection procedure is a training program. In the beginning of the program, participants may not be successful in entering the state of mind necessary to allow the messages from the loved one to come into consciousness. If the participants are not convinced that their loved ones are accessible and willing to communicate, they may give up on the program, becoming even more convinced that the person is unavailable or unwilling to communicate. Stage 2 counsels participants that if they are not convinced that the person in the afterlife can communicate, they should probably not begin the training. Their doubt may thwart the connection.

The online materials explain that their loved ones are alive, well, happy, and only a thought away. They are accessible and anxious to communicate. They briefly explain that the sense of presence people feel is as real as the senses of seeing and hearing. The Stage 2 materials go on to explain that communicating with loved ones in the afterlife will not hold them back from progressing. They in fact are anxious to connect.

This is what one experiencer wrote that her loved one said to her during her Self-Guided Afterlife Connection:

Tom tells me every Soul wants to connect. Some have
no one who validates how they tried to connect.
Eventually those may stop trying. Then those like Tom,
who knew I would never not notice, send a sign. The
person on this side of life acknowledges the sign, so the
person in spirit does something else. Tom says that the
more those in spirit do, the more we on the Earth plane
see, and they do more because we validated the
connection. And so on and so on.

The Stage 2 materials contain explanations to help people reject the
mistaken beliefs that communicating with loved ones in spirit is a sin or
that demons actually communicate with people when they connect with
the afterlife.

Learn to Relax the Conscious Mind

To have a connection with a loved one who has passed, the
participant must relax the conscious mind to receive the messages from
those in spirit. In Guided Afterlife Connections, bilateral stimulation
results in a change in the mind's structure that creates an openness to
messages from the greater reality. In the Self-Guided Afterlife
Connection process, the conscious mind is relaxed through hypnosis.

In Stages 3, 4, and 5, participants listen to meditation music through
a headset while I narrate a standard script to bring them into a hypnotic
trance. In Stage 6, the participants learn to put themselves into the
hypnotic trance with just the meditation music. In Stage 7, they put
themselves into the hypnotic trance without the aid of a narration or
music. After they have learned to put themselves into the hypnotic
trance, they are able to connect with their loved ones at anytime,
anyplace. As they practice over time, it becomes easier and easier to
make the connections at will.

Learn to Allow Free Unfoldment

After the participants have relaxed the conscious mind, they must
receive communication from loved ones in spirit by allowing the
messages to unfold naturally. However, our natural tendency is to want
to control what comes to us in the mind. People learned from infancy to
control their thoughts in order to meet challenges in the physical realm.
In an afterlife connection, participants must give up control and allow
those in the afterlife to unfold the connection. Relaxing control of
mental processes is an activity most people have never experienced. As
a result, the Self-Guided Afterlife Connection procedure trains them to

relinquish control and allow the communication to unfold as those in spirit want it to unfold. They are in charge.

The desire to control what happens during the Self-Guided Afterlife Connection Procedure is heightened because participants are anxious to have an afterlife connection, so they may try to make the connection happen by imagining their loved one's presence or calling out to their loved one or in some other way striving to create the connetion. To have a connection, they must learn to relax and allow the loved one in spirit to take control. Participants must learn to allow free unfoldment, in which messages from the loved one come into the person's consciousness without control, inhibition, or judgment

Participants learn about free unfoldment in Stage 3. They listen to narrations in which I guide them through the experience. In the background of the narrations, they listen to meditation music through headphones that alternates in volume between their ears, giving a mild bilateral stimulation. This bilateral stimulation doesn't have the strength to break down barriers in the mind that might result in exposing repressed memories or trauma.

The narrations with background music take participants through three exercises that help them understand what free unfoldment is and how to allow it to occur. After each exercise, participants write a journal of what happened during the exercise. The journals are submitted to me automatically via e-mail when they click on a "Submit" button. I read every journal and coach the participants in how to allow free unfoldment. For some, the unfoldment occurs quickly and naturally. Some, in fact, have an afterlife connection immediately. Others find it difficult to relax control and allow the unfoldment to happen. They require coaching and may repeat the Stage 3 activities several times.

In Stage 3, the narration takes the participant into a hypnotic state. The narration then asks them to imagine a very pleasant scene. There, they are to imagine a child. They are to say hello to the child and see what the response is. After they have finished that exercise, they are brought out of the trance and listen to this explanation:

> That was imagination. You intended to see a child and the child simply appeared. You spoke no words to make the child appear, and yet in an instant, a realistic child was created and an entire scene unfolded. You didn't have to draw or paint her, a brushstroke at a time. You didn't have to set up something to see a video or picture. You just intended it. That's a miracle. We take it for granted, but that is nothing short of astounding.

Now, what gender was the child? What was the color of
the child's skin? What color hair? What color clothing.
What was the child doing? What did the child say in
response? You have answers for all of those questions.
You experienced all of those details in your mind. But
you didn't plan any of that. You just intended to see a
child and have the child respond. You didn't think,
"Make the child a boy, 5 years old, with blonde hair,
wearing a striped shirt." Yet you experienced all of the
details about the child's gender, age, hair color, and
clothing. Where did all of those very clear details you
experienced come from?

That child and the scene came from the Source that
creates and sustains the universe. You may call the
source the Higher Power or God. When you intended to
see a child, you linked to the Source, the mind of God.
Your Higher Self is one with the Source. You asked,
and the Source gave you what you asked for in a more
marvelous way than you could have ever sketched or
painted yourself. The Source gave you the child, in
clothing, with a face, color of hair, actions, words, smile,
and everything else that wasn't in your simple request to
see a child. None of that came from you. That's called
unfoldment. It all unfolded from your Higher Self and
the Source of creation when you just intended to see a
child in that pleasant place.

Unfoldment comes from the Source, from our Higher
Self, from helpers, from guides, and from our loved ones
on the other side. To communicate with our loved ones
in spirit, with your guides, and with the Source, you
have to learn to <u>allow</u> unfoldment.

Stage 3 then continues with teaching the participant about free
unfoldment. In the second part of Stage 3, participants are asked to
engage in a daydream. The reason is that people are accustomed to
daydreaming, so it is a natural mental process they can perform easily.
However, daydreams are controlled activities. The person intends to be
in a scene and the Source unfolds the scene. For example, the person
imagines being with a friend at an amusement park. The source provides
the images of rides, the sounds, the feel of warmth in the sun, the
spontaneous words the person speaks. None of those details are planned.
They unfold naturally.

The person then takes control and manipulates the daydream through intention, making the next action in the daydream happen in the mind. The Source gives the person that new scene, with all of the embellishments and details the person didn't create, but which unfolded naturally. The person then takes control again and guides the daydream. This process of controlling what the person intends to happen, allowing unfoldment by the Source, taking control again with unfoldment following, and so on, continues through the entire daydream.

In this second part of Stage 3, the participants are taken into a hypnotic trance and asked to daydream, but not take control of the daydream as it unfolds. They start with a scene and allow it to unfold completely on its own. Once the daydream starts they do not intend for it to go in a direction, do not add a memory, do not change the content, and no other way control what happens. They allow the free unfoldment to occur throughout the experience. This is their practice in allowing the free unfoldment their loved ones will take control of to unfold the connection they want the person to have.

These are the instructions they hear in the narration:

> Now daydream. Let some pleasant place just come to you. It could be the place where you just were. It could be another place. Look around. As you look, listen for anything, smell whatever comes, feel the air. Let the scene unfold. Don't control it. Don't imagine or intend anything beyond just being in that scene.
>
> Move around the scene in your mind. Experience whatever comes to you as you notice what you see, hear, smell, or sense. You're learning to let things unfold freely.
>
> Stay as long as you want. Let things unfold freely, naturally. When you're finished, count from one to five and become more awake as you count.

They emerge from the trance and listen to this explanation:

> You were daydreaming about being in a pleasant place, but nearly all of it came from unfoldment given to you by the Source. You control the intention. You intend to be in the scene. You intend to see the scene. You intend to hear the sounds. You intend to feel the feelings. But you don't create the experience. You don't make whatever you experienced. With a simple intention, not spoken in words, the Source gives you an entire

experience as though you were actually in that pleasant
place. When you daydream or imagine, you're simply
asking for the experience. The experience comes from
the Source. That's unfoldment.

After listening to that explanation, participants write what happened
in their journal. The journal is submitted to me via e-mail. I encourage
them or coach them through learning how to allow free unfoldment
without control. I may ask them to repeat the activity if they haven't
been able to relinquish control.

At this stage, often an afterlife connection will occur spontaneously.
It then unfolds by itself.

In the third and final part of Stage 3, a narration takes the
participants into another trance. It begins with this explanation:

You're going to a very pleasant place again. There,
you'll practice allowing things to unfold, naturally. You
won't control what unfolds once you go there. When
you're there, you'll watch and notice. Be aware of
everything, but don't imagine or remember anything.
Just let whatever comes come to you, without your
effort.

After they have been led into the trance, they receive this instruction:

Now you're in that pleasant place again, or some other
very pleasant place. Look around. Notice what you see,
but don't try to make anything come. Let whatever
comes come to you without intending anything. Smell
smells. Hear sounds. As something comes, notice it.
Let your attention stay on it without making it anything.
Let things unfold without controlling them. Don't
imagine or intend or bring up a memory. Just allow
things to unfold.

[The narration pauses for a while. The meditation
music continues. Then the narration resumes.]

Very good.

In a moment, when I tell you to, ask "Is there anyone
here?" Then ask, "Does anyone have a message for
me?" Then be still. Let whatever unfolds come. It
might be a response. It might be silence. Notice that
and let whatever comes come. Respond if you hear or
sense something. Then be still again and wait. Notice

whatever impressions, feelings, sights, or sounds come.
Stay as long as you want. When you're finished, count
from one to five and become more awake as you count.
Now, ask "Is there anyone here?" Then ask "Does
anyone have a message for me?"

The narration stops and the music plays while the participants
imagine the scene. After a while, the narration takes them out of the
trance and they listen to this explanation:

Whatever came to you was unfoldment. Messages
unfold. When you ask, you may receive, and what you
receive will not be something you've created. It comes
from the Source, your Higher Self, or from someone you
love on the other side of life. If nothing unfolded for
you yet, you just need more experiences and more
confidence they will come. This training program will
help you.

You should have a sense of what unfoldment is now. It
originates from the Source when you intend to have an
experience. It is filled with sights, sounds, impressions,
and actions you didn't specify. The Source gives you
the experience. Your conscious mind doesn't create the
experience. You just intend to have an experience.
Your intention is the act of asking the Source for what
you want.

When people say, I don't know if that was a message
from my loved one or my imagination, what they don't
realize is that very little of imagination comes from
them. What comes from them is just the intention.
What they experience comes from the Source and from
loved ones on the next plane of life.

The participants journal what happened to them. I coach them
through allowing free unfoldment if they were still taking control. If
they have not yet learned to relax and relinquish control, I ask them to
repeat the exercises in Stage 3. This ability to allow free unfoldment so
the Source, their guides, or their loved ones in spirit can take control and
unfold their message is critical to having afterlife connections. If they
continue to control by trying to imagine their loved one there or changing
the scene hoping that will make a connection occur or any other control
over what comes to them, they will thwart the unfoldment that would
come to them naturally, without their intervention.

The signs that participants are allowing free unfoldment are very clear. They receive "dream stuff" that is unintended and unplanned scenes, faces, bodily sensations, words, and actions by people they may or may not know. In a sense, they are dreaming while completely awake. Dreams are free unfoldment because the conscious mind is anesthetized by the sleep state.

In the early stages, very often clear, distinctive people come into view without speaking. Often the participant sees a loved one or deceased pet in in the distance or walking by. It seems that in the early stage, the participant is still learning how to allow the free unfoldment that will eventually result in extensive, vivid communication, but in the early stages it is dampened by the person's being engaged in what is coming without expectation. When they finally allow free unfoldment, it is the first time they have experienced it outside of a dream state. The experience is enthralling.

Experience a State of Mind Infused with Feelings Love and Compassion

The Induced After-Death Connections and Guided Afterlife Connections focus on disturbing or traumatic memories before the connections occur. When the disturbing nature of the memories is reduced through bilateral stimulation, the afterlife connection begins to unfold. It seems that the memories are disturbing because of the great love the participant feels for the person in spirit. When the disturbing nature of the memory is removed, what is left is the love that precipitated the feelings of grief. From that love, the connection emerges.

In the Self-Guided Afterlife Connection, Stage 4 takes the participants into trance and has them envision a place of great beauty. In that place of great beauty, there is only love. They are guided into feeling great love and then to focus that love on the person in spirit. These are the instructions:

> I'm going to count from five to one, and with each
> count, you're going to go deeply into the subconscious
> part of you that is where deep love is. There, you will
> feel only love, the unconditional love of the Higher
> Power. 5, Sink into the love, deeply, feel the love for
> your friends, 4 more deeply, feel the love for your family
> and pets, 3 more deeply, feel the love for all of
> humankind, 2 more deeply, feel the love for everyone
> who needs love at this moment, 1 more deeply, feel the
> love for those you love who have passed away.

You're weightless now, floating downward into the
warm, loving place inside you where you love
everything and everyone, and there you are loved,
unconditionally. You've never felt such overwhelming,
consuming love. You can feel yourself floating into the
warm, wonderful part of you where love is. You're like
a baby nestled into a fuzzy, warm blanket. And in the
comfort, safety, and love you feel, you can relax more
and more, with no worries, no burdens. They're all
lifted from you by the love that enfolds you.

Let go and relax. Let yourself sink into the love. Get
ready to let go completely, even more. Here it comes,
now, go deeper and deeper just letting go, relaxing,
melting. And relax completely.

The narration then has them imagine a place of great beauty, where
this love is. The reason is that the participant will be able to come back
to this place and enter the state of mind quickly and naturally. Charles
Tart explains that when a person recalls the state of consciousness in
which the person experienced something, the person brings back the
entire state of consciousness and re-experiences it (1969). The
experience of being in this place of great beauty, infused with love,
becomes a state of consciousness. When the participant recalls this place
of great beauty later, all of the pleasant feelings, sights, memories of
connections, and feelings of love emerge as a state of consciousness.
Entering that state of consciousness will allow the connection to occur
quickly. This part of the narration helps them create this place of great
beauty where love is, in their minds:

Now, you are going into a place of great beauty that is
inside you. It might be in a little house, in a forest, or by
a stream with flowers, or in a marble palace, wherever
you feel it should be. Go there now.

It is the place of love. Be in that place of great beauty
filled with the love that pours over you. You may sense
it or feel its protection and warmth. You may see its
surroundings, or smell wonderful smells. You may hear
beautiful singing in the distance. You may feel a breeze
or the warmth like a sun. It's a wonderful, comfortable
place because it's full of love.

The love in the place of great beauty is then associated with the person in spirit with whom the participant wants to connect. This is the narration:

> Now, in that place of great beauty, you sense that there are people and pets close by. They are the people and pets you know who have passed away. They've never left you. They are always with you. You know they're there when you feel their presence.

> As you stay in that place of great beauty, you're going to remember that person or pet who has passed away. Remember images of them with you when they were on Earth. It's like you're looking through a picture album, one picture after another. Remember them with you.

After the participant is in this state of consciousness, filled with feelings of love and memories of the person in spirit, the person is ready to have the connection. The narration guides them into the connection:

> Now, in that place of great beauty where love is, there's an opening. It's full of love, so you may see it glow with love. In that opening, you feel the presence of that person or pet who has passed away. It's the opening to the afterlife, and they're there waiting to greet you now.

> Step forward through the opening. You're with them now, even if you can't see them. You sense them. It isn't imagination or remembering. They're here. Relax and now let whatever happens happen. You may sense them. You may see them, or hear them, or feel their touch. You know they're here with you now.

> Now, greet them and tell them how you feel about them. Then wait for any impression of a response. Let whatever comes come. Carry on a dialogue. When you feel you're finished, come out of the experience by counting from one to five.

The narration ends by having them bring themselves out of the experience. The reason is that early in the development of this procedure, I learned that some people have a connection very quickly and easily. The narration's bringing them out of the experience actually interrupts an ongoing communication. As a result, they are asked to stay in the trance state as long as they want to. They then may participate in the connection for an extended period of time. The meditation music continues for another 30 minutes so they can have a connection for as long as they want and count themselves back to a normal state of consciousness by counting backwards from five to one.

During Stages 3 and 4, most people have a connection with someone in spirit. It may not be the person they expected, and the first connections may not be deep and full of experiences. Deeper and longer connections emerge later.

Stage 5: For People Having Difficulty

Stage 5 is designed for people who may not have been successful in having a connection in Stages 3 or 4. People who have had a connection in Stages 3 or 4 are encouraged to go on to Stage 6, but may go through Stage 5 if they want to.

Stage 5 has the participants go through a modified version of the method of encouraging an afterlife connection developed by the medium Phil G. that he calls "coffee time." In this activity, the person imagines sitting at a table with a chair at the opposite side of the table. Before the chair on the table is a cup of coffee, perhaps the favorite cup that belonged to the loved one in spirit. The person is to imagine or daydream a dialogue with the person in spirit. During the imagined dialogue, the talk may develop into an afterlife connection.

The purpose of having the person engage in this activity is to help them practice having a daydream with this person and to see whether the daydream might develop into an afterlife connection. Often, the participants have a connection during this daydream. At times, they believe at least part of the dialogue is a connection.

That daydream exercise is followed by a second activity in which the participant is taken into trance using the same induction script used for Stage 4. However, after the induction, the person imagines another daydream with the person in spirit. This activity is an effort to see whether being in the relaxed hypnotic trance may enable people who have not yet had a connection experience one. Often, people who were not successful in Stages 3 and 4 are successful in this activity.

Stages 6 and 7

Stages 6 and 7 are for people who have successfully had connections with loved ones in the previous stages. These stages have the person practice entering the hypnotic trance through self-hypnosis and experience connections. In Stage 6, the participant listens to the meditation music only, with no narration taking them into the hypnotic state. They induce themselves using a brief version of the hypnosis script explained in the Stage 6 materials.

In Stage 7, the participants are asked to take themselves into the hypnotic trance without a narration and without meditation music. They simply sit quietly and use the self-hypnosis procedure to take themselves into trance, go to the place of great beauty where love is, and communicate with their loved one.

Stage 8

Stage 8 explains how the participant can become sensitive to the sense of presence that indicates the loved one in spirit is nearby and wants to communicate. With their ability to sit quietly without music or assistance and enter the state of consciousness in which the connections occur, the person can stop when he or she feels the sense of presence and have a spontaneous dialogue with the person in spirit.

Results of Use of the Procedure

In one study of 22 participants who had completed at least Stage 4 training, 86% described having afterlife connections.

The afterlife connections involve extended conversations, taking tours and trips in the afterlife, holding hands walking along a path or the beach, hugs, kisses, riding horses, swimming together, and a wide range of other activities.

In some of the connections, participants met the Higher Selves of people living on the Earth plane, guides, and helpers. Often, they meet people they knew little about when they were on the Earth plane or they had forgotten about. Pets are very common in the connections.

Some participants now interact with their loved ones every day. The connections become deeper and filled with metaphysical dialogues and activities. One woman's husband on the other side assists people who are newly passed or who are involved in a near-death experience and will return to the Earth plane. He takes her with him on the missions and she experiences from the other side what we hear about from people who have died or who have had near-death experiences.

Participants explain that their lives change as a result of the connections. Some have written that they now can have the relationship with their loved one that they couldn't when the loved one was alive on the Earth plane because of difficulties between them.

Some participants have also used the procedure to connect with the Higher Selves of people unable to communicate who are still alive on the

Earth plane, and the higher selves of people with whom they have a relationship on the Earth plane to get insights into their relationships.

Validations

Validations of the reality of the connections are common. Following are just two examples.

A woman had a Self-Guided Afterlife Connection with her grandfather in spirit. Afterward, when she told her grandmother, still on the Earth plane, about her experience, her grandmother asked the woman to see if she could connect with her grandmother's mother the next time she had a session. When the woman had her next connection with her grandfather, she asked him whether she could connect with her grandmother's mother. Immediately a young girl appeared, around 16, and the woman having the experience heard the name "Mabel" three times. When the woman ended her session and went to her grandmother, she explained that she didn't connect with her grandmother's mother, but a young girl appeared and she heard the name "Mabel" three times. The grandmother exclaimed immediately, "Oh, that was my sister Mabel. She died when she was 16." The woman who had the connection had known nothing about Mabel.

Another woman had a session connecting with a friend in spirit when she had the clear image of a young girl in an apron cooking. She recognized the young girl as the daughter of a friend. The daughter had passed into spirit in a car accident. The woman heard the girl say, "I miss my mom." The girl was engaged in cooking, wearing a checkered apron, and the woman had the feeling the girl loved cooking with her mother. Then she saw the girl making "rollups," dough spread out and filled with some meat, such as lobster. But what she saw surprised her. The girl was putting jalapeño peppers in the rollup. The woman was taken aback. She had never heard of putting peppers in a rollup. After the session, the woman spoke with the girl's mother, telling her about her connection. The mother said, yes they loved to cook together, and her daughter would wear an apron like the one the woman had seen in her connection. The woman who had the experience said there was something odd, however. The daughter was making rollups by putting jalapeño peppers in them. The mother said "Oh yes, making rollups with jalapeño peppers was one of our favorite things to do."

Biography

R. Craig Hogan, Ph.D., is director of the Center for Spiritual Understanding, devoted to helping people develop spiritual understanding through afterlife connections. He is the author of *Your Eternal Self*, presenting the scientific evidence that the mind is not confined to the brain, the afterlife is a reality, people's minds are linked, and the mind affects the physical world.

Craig co-authored *Induced After-Death Communication: A New Therapy for Healing Grief and Trauma* with Allan Botkin, Psy.D., and *Guided Afterlife Connections: They Come to Change Lives* with Rochelle Wright, M.S. He is the editor of *Afterlife Communications: 16 Methods, 85 True Accounts*, containing accounts of afterlife communications written by the presenters at the Academy for Spiritual and Consciousness Studies 38th annual conference.

He is on the boards of the Academy for Spiritual and Consciousness Studies, Association for Evaluation and Communication of Evidence for Survival, and American Society for Standards in Mediumship and Psychical Investigation.

Craig is the author of two textbooks on business writing, a personality styles survey, and a book teaching public school administrators how to work with teachers to maintain healthy work relationships while improving their teaching.

Bibliography

Simpson, M. (2011, October 30). A Sister's Euology for Steve Jobs. New York, NY: *New York Times*.

Beals, G. (1999). *The Biography of Thomas Edison.* From http://www.thomasedison.com/biography.html.

Lawrence, M. and Repede, E. (2013). The Incidence of Deathbed Communications and Their Impact on the Dying Process. *American Journal of Hospice & Palliative Medicine*, from http://ajh.sagepub.com/content/early/2012/12/07/1049909112467529.a bstract.

Monroe, R. (1977). *Journeys Out of the Body*. Anchor Press.

Wright, R. and Hogan, R. C. (2010). *Guided Afterlife Connections: They Come to Change Lives*. Normal, IL: Greater Reality Publications.

Hogan, R.C. (2012). "The Resolution of Grief by Guided Afterlife Connections." From http://newsletter.guidedafterlifeconnections.com/SUDS_Article.htm.

Schlitz, M. (2014). "Experimenter Effects and Replication in Psi Research." Noetic Now: Institute of Noetic Sciences. From http://www.noetic.org/blog/experimenter-effects-and-replication-in-psi-resear/

Tart, C. (1969). *Altered States of Consciousness: A Book of Readings*. New York, NY: Wiley.

Graham, P. (n.d.). "Coffee Time." From http://www.youtube.com/watch?v=jN4SOjwY2Mw.

Meditation Connections

Maria Pe, Esq.

Abstract

The paper describes Marie Pe's background, the murder of her two sons, her search to find a way to contact them, and the resulting meditation connections she learned to make. It explains how she developed her meditation connection abilities and some of the encounters she has had with her sons living in the Upper Realm, her guide Michael, her animal guide Black Panther, her sons' companion Dillon, and others she has met on her meditation journeys to be with her sons. It ends with an explanation of how to go into a shifting consciousness meditation.

Meditation Connections

by Maria Pe, Esq.

In this article, I speak about communicating with loved ones on the other side through meditation. Because I'm a lawyer by training, I want to start off with a few disclaimers. First, I am not an expert on meditation, spirit communication or afterlife studies. I've never done any scientific research or studies on those topics, and I'm not a teacher or practitioner either. So I think it's important for you to know that I'm speaking only from my own personal perspective and my own personal experiences. I'm a mother who lost both of my sons, my only children, and wanted desperately to continue my relationship with them.

I want to talk first a little bit about my background and my human persona because it was my focus for the first 49 years of my life. I was born in Manila, Philippines, to a Filipina mother and a Chinese father. My family immigrated to North America in 1966 and I spent most of my childhood growing up in the San Diego area. I had what most people would consider to be a mainstream upbringing and I was taught to do well in school and to excel at whatever I did. When I was nine years old, I was introduced to tennis and because I had a natural ability for the game, my father quickly turned me into a competitive tennis player. I started playing tennis tournaments almost every weekend, so my parents stopped taking us to church and we became devout followers of what I like to call the church of tennis.

In my senior year of high school I was accepted to Harvard University. So I set off for the east coast and spent the next four years at Harvard, earning my bachelor's degree. I eventually returned to San Diego after I had had one too many cold winters, and I attended law school at the University of San Diego. I practiced law for several years and did a lot of training and consulting in the corporate world. I was marching down the path of achievement and I was deeply entrenched in the physical, material world.

Like a lot of people, I was looking for something to be passionate about and I thought that I would be able to find it in my career and in my professional pursuits. I mean, after all, that was what I had been raised to believe—that it was all about achieving, performing and acquiring. But time passed and I did not really find any lasting passion in my work or other external activities, so I resigned myself to the idea that maybe that was just the way it was going to be for me.

But then my sons came into my life. It was not until their births that I could say that I really found deep meaning in my life. My first son, Sean, was born on May 9, 1996 and my second son, Kyle, was born on February 4, 1998. I was completely surprised and overwhelmed with the depth of love I felt for them the moment each one of them was born. They became the passion in my life and they were the source of tremendous love and happiness for me. I had them here with me for a little more than 13 and 15 years, less than a third of my entire life.

On June 21, 2011, they were killed. It was a night that they were with their father who shared custody of them with me. It was their father who killed them, and who then took his own life. It was the unimaginable, the inconceivable. But there it was, the beginning of my journey.

Sean and Kyle came to me very soon after they were killed. As you can imagine, I was in a profound state of shock on that day, June 21, so my memory of that day and the weeks following may be a little foggy. But I do remember that they came to me, and I intuitively knew that it was them even though I had never experienced anything like it before. How they came to me initially was through color. When I would close my eyes, my entire field of vision, which was normally just blackness, was filled with neon green and electric blue light. I knew it was them and so I just started talking to those lights. I guess you could say that it was communication through desperation.

I think that's how I got through the first several days, and how I managed to put together the memorial celebration for my sons. But when everything was done and I eventually had to return to my own home, I was at a loss as to what to do next. **I had no religious practice and I had only vague spiritual beliefs.**

I remember one day in particular when I was sitting at my desk at home and I was completely lost and in utter desolation. The grief and sadness were overwhelming. But I also had a feeling that there must be something more than just the grief and getting through the grieving process. I had questions that I needed answers to, two burning questions. The first question was, where did my sons go? And the second question was, how can I continue to have a relationship with them? I knew intuitively that they were "somewhere," that they still existed, and that there must be a way for me to still have a relationship with them. For me, it was simply not going to be acceptable to NOT have a relationship with them.

So as I sat there with these two burning questions, but feeling absolutely lost and helpless as to how to get answers to them, the name "Marcie" suddenly popped into my head. I thought about it for a minute. Then I remembered that my friend Shannon had emailed me during the first week after my sons' deaths to tell me that her sister Marcie had "checked" on the boys and that Marcie had said that they were doing OK. Because I had been in such a fog during that timeframe, I hadn't really thought about that message. But now, as I started to remember it, I intuitively knew that Marcie could help me. And I say intuitively because I did not really know Marcie. I think I had met her briefly one time when she came to San Diego to visit Shannon, but I didn't remember her or what she looked like. And I certainly didn't know anything about what she did. So this feeling that I had that Marcie could help me wasn't rational, and it wasn't logical, but I had no other place to turn for help.

The next day, I had a phone conversation with Marcie. In that first conversation, Marcie told me: As humans, we need to balance our four "bodies"—the physical, intellectual, emotional, and spiritual bodies. The spiritual body is how we connect to the other realm. We need to get your spiritual body balanced with the others, so that it is not dominated. And you need to trust that your spiritual body is as real as the other bodies.

This was the first time that I had heard about the concept of four bodies and about balancing them. I started to realize that for most of my life, I had been focused primarily on the physical and intellectual aspects of myself, and somewhat on my emotional aspect, but my spiritual body had been sorely neglected.

Dr. Elisabeth Kubler-Ross said this about our four quadrants: "Every human being consists of four quadrants, a physical, an emotional, an intellectual, and a spiritual/intuitive quadrant. Spiritually we are OK. The only quadrant you never have to work with is your spiritual quadrant. It is within you and the most important reason it is not emerging is that it is blocked. If you live in harmony between the four quadrants, you will not get sick, you will always be whole. You are born from God and your spiritual quadrant is given to you as a gift. The only thing that blocks you from using it is your own negativity."

After my conversation with Marcie, I started to feel a little more hopeful and she agreed to help me. First, she gave me some homework. She asked me to start doing simple meditations as often as I could throughout the day. She said that I should sit in a quiet place, close my eyes, and listen and feel. She told me not to judge anything, just listen and feel, then afterwards, write down everything I could remember.

This is what my first meditation was like: What I heard: leaves rustling in the wind; wind; leaves brushing up against the planter; small planes; large planes; a bird chirping; children's voices; a car; clanging; machinery beeping; buzzing fly; wind chimes; a dog barking; birds wailing; helicopter. What I felt: the breeze; chills; warmth of the sun; the boys thru colors (deep purple with blue veins, shots of neon green with a blue dot; bright orange; many colors); energy from the sun; calm; peaceful; serene; comfortable.

As I continued to do these short meditations, I was surprised at how quickly I moved from hearing to feeling. This is what one of my later meditations was like: What I heard—birds tweeting, beeping machinery, drum beats, planes, buzzing insects. What I felt—sorrow, loss, stomach upset, sadness; then Sean and Kyle hugging and touching me, lots of purple with lightning streaks of neon purple. Kyle's blue circle inside of Sean's green circle. Talked but can't recall much. I love you! You will help me and stay with me, right boys? "Yes, momma we are always with you." Sean says, "You are doing so good, Mom." Felt Kyle in my lap, touching my face, felt his strong hugs and soft skin. Could not feel my body. Tried to tell my mom, I'm sorry I have not connected. I miss you, Mom. I can't think of any two better people to take care of Sean and Kyle—you and Auntie Lina. We are all so blessed with each other. Told Sean and Kyle, "All I need is you two. You will show me the way, you will help me on my journey, so I will know what is right, right boys?"

"Yes, momma, we will. We will always be with you and we will all be together in this realm and when you come to us."

As I think back on those early meditations, I see how helpful it was to start out with focusing on what I could hear. I think it gave my intellectual, rational mind something to do, and so it helped me to avoid too much thinking and instead go into feeling much faster.

The following month I travelled to Northern California to do my work with Marcie. I like to call it spiritual boot camp. It was very intensive and it was totally new to me. Marcie did some emotional body healing on me, which basically consisted of releasing emotions that were trapped in my body. She also worked on clearing and balancing my chakras. I don't have time today to talk in detail about those processes, but I am happy to give more information to anyone who is interested in those aspects of my experience.

So now I want to talk about learning how to do journey meditations. My first journey meditation was a visit to Animal Realm, a place where animals reside in spirit form. Now remember, again, I had no experience with this type of activity. I had tried a handful of times, in my earlier life, to meditate, but I always just seemed to fall asleep. So I really wasn't sure what to expect in these journey meditations. These meditations were guided. In other words, Marcie led me through guided imagery so I could learn to see in my mind's eye where I was going.

This is what I wrote after my first journey into Animal Realm: Felt like I didn't really "go" anywhere. Felt like I had a commentator with me, lots of thoughts flashing through my head. Saw a meadow in Sequoia and the big tree that the boys had stood in front of. Went down into that tree. I seemed to drop down into a lush jungle-type setting, but it was not clear. Fleeting shadows of a male lion, but very vague. Saw mostly black/dark. Too much self-criticism going on?

As you can imagine, I was a little disappointed with that first experience. But one of the things that I really appreciated about Marcie is that she did not give me a lot of detailed instructions or lecture me, or tell me what I should or should not be experiencing. She just led me along and let me have my own experience. So the next time we went to Animal Realm, which was very soon after my first visit, this is the experience that I had: Started in the meadow, walked down the path to the large tree and climbed in, then down. Landed in a lush tropical jungle again. Saw a yellow snake that scared me, saw a black panther, then a tiger. The black panther stayed with me. We laid down on the grass. I asked him if he was my guide, and he said yes. He let me pet him for a while, and he stayed with me. Then he said he had to go. He jumped onto a high tree limb, then said again that he had to go. I said, no, wait, don't leave me, and I started to cry. I felt so alone and scared.

I made my way back to the tree, climbed up and out, and walked back up the path. I was OK by then.

I was really surprised by this experience and how "real" it seemed to me. I was also surprised at how quickly and easily it happened. The next journey meditation I did was a visit to Fairy Realm. In the interests of time, I won't go into detail about that journey now, but I will just say that it was a very interesting and beautiful experience.

So let's talk about my journeys to the Upper Realm and how I learned to communicate with Sean and Kyle. After getting my feet wet, so to speak, in the animal and fairy realms, I was ready to go to the Upper Realm. Marcie told me that I would not be meeting the boys right away, but that I first needed to create the special place where we would meet.

Again, it was a guided meditation. I started in a meadow and walked down a path to a well. I stood next to the well and dropped down any worries or troubles I was feeling. Then I walked up a path towards the edge of a cliff. At the cliff's edge was a cloud. I stepped onto the cloud and it lifted me higher and higher, floating upward until I reached a garden. I stepped into the garden and walked to a bench where I met my spirit guide. We walked a short distance from the garden and that is where I created the sanctuary that would become my meeting place with my boys.

It was in my next visit to the Upper Realm that I got to meet with Sean and Kyle. It was an amazing experience, and, as you can imagine, it was very emotional. I went to the Upper Realm in the same way I had the first time, from the meadow to the cliff and onto the cloud, to the garden and into the sanctuary. A few moments after I entered the sanctuary, the boys appeared. And they looked the way they had when they were in the physical world. I hugged and kissed them, and I could feel them, their hair, their skin, their faces. And we talked. They assured me that they are doing well where they are, and that I would be OK. I was totally blown away that I could do this!

After I finished my work with Marcie and returned home, I developed a very specific routine for my journeys. I would lie down on the floor in my bedroom, put on earphones to listen to rhythmic drumming, do my journey meditation for 20 minutes, then record everything in my journal. Over the course of the next several months, I went on these journeys to the Upper Realm every three days to be with my sons, to see them, touch them and talk to them. They constantly gave me assurances that they are doing well. They also told me again and again that they are with me, that they are helping me and guiding me, and that our love has not diminished in any way, but has actually gotten stronger and brighter.

These journeys were very comforting to me, and the experiences were very powerful, but there was still a part of me that doubted and questioned them. In truth, I was still skeptical about what I was experiencing. At one point I asked the boys, "Am I making all of this up?" They responded, "Yeah, Mom, you are, but who are 'you'? You are part of the whole, the One, where all thought originates, so if 'you' are making this up, it is real." What was I going to say to that? They are in a lot better position than me to know, right? So I just tried to accept my experiences for what they were. I mean, how could I decide whether my experiences in the Upper Realm were any less real than my experiences down here?

There were also times when I was unfocused in my journeys and my thoughts would go all over the place. So sometimes I would get critical and judgmental about myself. But Sean and Kyle would just assure me that it was OK, and they would tell me to just let my experience at that moment be whatever it was.

And then there were those journeys that left me full of awe, wonder and gratitude. In one of my visits, they told me: "Be open and know that we are all one, everyone is connected. Remember the feelings of unconditional love and compassion that we pass on to you, that we infuse you with. See all of the people that you encounter in the same way, with love and compassion. That is the challenge of the human condition."

Sean and Kyle really kept me going. As much as I wanted at times for my life here to end, they kept me going. In one of my journeys, Sean said to me: "Mom, you know you will be with us soon. It feels like time passes slowly there, but here it is fast, we will be here waiting for you, but you still have a lot to do there. We are doing our work here and you are doing your work there. You will see, someday you will know what we know, you will know as much as we do and you will understand. So keep doing what feels right. Trust yourself, Mom."

It was a very challenging process, but I was learning how to trust myself and how to honor my intuition. That can be pretty tough for someone with a very logical and analytical mind, not to mention being a lawyer who is used to proof and evidence. I was allowing my spiritual and intuitive body to develop, but I was also trying to keep it balanced with my intellectual body which still needed to be fed too. So I was also reading and learning as much as I could about the afterlife, and staying open to the work of mediums, past life regression and soul planning. And I think what ultimately helped me reach my strong belief in the reality of the Upper Realm was the unexpected validation I got from a medium.

An important point that I want to make about my experience is that I don't think it's something that is limited to me. I believe that anyone can do this. Just like Dr. Elisabeth Kubler-Ross said, spiritually we are OK; your spiritual quadrant is within you; it is a gift given to you; and the only thing that blocks you from using it is your own negativity.

For me, journey meditation is what I was led to learn in order to communicate with my sons. Journey meditation is what worked for me. I think it's also what saved me and led me to greater truths which have ultimately kept me going.

From everything I have learned and experienced, I know that there is a much greater and larger plan for our lives. We are not privy to all of the details of the plan; otherwise, there would be no purpose for our human learning experience. But with that knowledge and with trust in spirit, I have been able to keep doing things on Earth to honor my sons and to honor our purpose for being here.

I made a promise to Sean and Kyle that I will keep trying, no matter how hard it is at times to keep going, I will keep trying, and I will not let them down. So, ironically, what pulls me to the other side is exactly the same thing that keeps me here—my sons. So I know I am still meant to be here and to do more work here.

Part of my work has been and will continue to be sharing my story so that others might be helped by it. In April 2012, when I started getting the message to write a book about my experiences in the Upper Realm, I knew it was a divine directive because writing a book was the last thing on my mind. It was barely ten months since my sons' deaths and I was not interested in sharing the most intimate depths of my grief publicly. But I knew, intuitively once again, that it was something I had to do.

The book is called Journey To The Upper Realm: How I Survived the Deaths of My Sons and Learned to Communicate With Them on The Other Side. But I also think of it as, "How my sons spent a full year proving to me the existence of the afterlife and what we all really are— divine, eternal beings with the innate ability to connect to each other in spirit."

Shifting Consciousness Meditation

Get in a comfortable position on the floor or on soft furniture, laying down or sitting up. Once you are comfortable, close your eyes. Take a deep breath and exhale slowly. Take another deep breath, hold it for a moment, then exhale slowly. Continue breathing deeply and with each breath you take, feel all the tension of the day and the week leaving your body. With each breath, feel your body becoming lighter.

Now focus your thoughts on your third eye chakra. Feel yourself coming out of your third eye. See your physical body resting comfortably as you float above it. Know that your physical body will be fine, as part of you is outside of it. Notice the cord attached to your Spirit body and your physical body. This cord keeps you connected to your physical body at all times. At any time during this exercise you can follow that cord back to your body.

Now from your spirit body, look around the room you are in. When you are comfortable that your physical body is fine and that you are safe, walk around the room. (pause) Now expand your consciousness to see the entire building that you are in. Feel free to walk around. Expand your consciousness further so that you are now floating above the building. Notice the roof, the yard, the landscaping. See the entire building as a bird does. (pause) Now expand your consciousness further, rising higher, until you see the entire neighborhood. (Focus on certain landmarks in the area). Now rise even higher. See the land for miles around your house, its hills or rivers, mountains or seashore. (pause) Continue to raise yourself until you see the outline of the entire country you live in, perhaps bordered by land and ocean. (pause) Continue to expand your consciousness, raising yourself until you see the Earth floating like a ball in the vast Universe. See the Earth getting smaller as you expand your consciousness and your focus even further out into space. (pause)

Now, shift your consciousness so you are focusing on the Earth again, moving closer to it. It grows so you see its outline but you can now make out geographical features. Continue to focus in on the Earth so that now you see the outline of your country again, bordered by land or mountains or sea. (pause) Continue to shift your consciousness back down until you see the surrounding states or provinces and the features of the landscape. (pause) Continue down until you see your state or province and then your city again. Continue closing in until you see the neighborhood. (pause) Now you see your building from just above again. Notice the roof, the surrounding yard, the landscaping. (pause) Shift your focus inside the building.

Walk into the room you started in. Notice your body. See that your physical body is fine. It is resting, waiting for you to re-enter it. Move to your body. Take a deep breath and merge back with your physical shell. Continue to take slow deep breaths. With each breath, feel your body again. Feel your breath enter and exit your lungs, feel your heart beat. When you are ready, open your eyes.

Biography

Maria Pe, Esq., was born in Manila, Philippines to a Filipina mother and Chinese father. Her family emigrated to North America in 1966 and she spent most of her childhood growing up in the San Diego area. She earned her bachelor's degree from Harvard University and law degree from the University of San Diego. She practiced law for several years and did much training and consulting in the corporate world. Today, she is Chief Deputy Tax Collector for the County of San Diego.

After her sons were murdered by their father, Maria found a way to connect with them through meditation. She wrote her book, *Journey to the Upper Realm*, describing her striving to find a way to communicate with her sons and finding it in meditation.

Repair & Reattachment Grief Therapy

Rochelle Wright, M.S.

Abstract

This paper describes a Repair & Reattachment grief therapy protocol called Guided Afterlife Connections. It explains that the work is done by state-licensed psychotherapists who are not mediums, and that the difference between the psychotherapist using this protocol and a medium is that the information comes through the connection to the person the psychotherapist is working with and the person tells the psychotherapist what they are getting. The psychotherapist is just as surprised as the client. It explains that the Repair & Reattachment protocol opens the portal to the afterlife connection and that the therapists trained in the procedure have the skills, heart and disposition to do this work but it is the "afterlife" or the "Wonderful Source," that makes the connection happen. The paper goes on to explain the protocol. It takes 5-6 hours in one session. The client comes for one day only. It is positive and healing. It reduces sadness and can reduce other disturbing emotions that the client has been carrying around in his or her thoughts, memories and body. It has been 98.5 percent positive, good and healing for the clients. They also can get direction and information about their current life.

Repair & Reattachment Grief Therapy

by Rochelle Wright

I have designed a protocol called Repair & Reattachment which is a grief repair-and-reattachment protocol that is definitely "think different: out of the box." As a general rule, licensed psychotherapists don't work with their clients to connect with the afterlife. I am not a medium; I'm a licensed therapist. The information comes to the client, not to me, and I write what is coming across so my client /experiencer can have a copy when we are finished.

I have the skills, the disposition and the heart to do this work but it is the afterlife or "the Wonderful Source," or spirit— whatever is the appropriate word for you to use—that makes this happen. Call it what you want; it's happening in the most delightful way. It's not me. I am just a tool or conduit; I just show up for this healing experience to happen.

I never know what's going to happen. We just have to see what happens. But it's been good and positive and healing in 98.5 percent of the people I've worked with. And in the other cases, their sadness has been reduced.

The many therapists I trained in the U.S. and abroad are getting the same connections. This is not unique to me. As long as they follow the protocol I've designed, their clients are connecting. It's all about energy and where the therapist's heart is. It is a simple process, but it requires a seasoned, licensed therapist with a spiritual inclination.

It's pretty exciting work. It is done in a psychotherapeutic setting. The protocol takes four to five hours or longer. Never have these clients/experiencers been able to work with their grief, sadness or complicated grief for a whole day and tell someone their story and have the traumatic points targeted without someone's interfering or interjecting their own thoughts and feelings into the conversation. This protocol allows the therapist to let the client tell their story.

The Repair & Reattachment protocol opens a portal to the afterlife or this "wonderful source" as I call it in my book. The deceased person targeted needs to be gone for a minimum of one year. I have worked with clients when the deceased has been gone for over 50 years, and some come through in a foreign language that the experiencer recognizes. This method appears to resolve sadness, grief, anger, and unresolved issues that were apparent when the deceased was alive. This is very healing for the client/experiencer. This "Wonderful Source" in many cases, gives helpful information for the client/experiencer on how to proceed, evolve, and move on.

So, they come to change lives if the client/experiencer really listens and really hears it. That is the key!

This work re-establishes the connection and is helpful for the feelings of being "cut off" and the suffering and pain that goes with the loss of the deceased person. This work re-establishes the connection! The objective is to let people know this wonderful, healing, cutting edge therapy is now available. It not only relieves grief and sadness, but changes people's lives for the better. It allows them to connect with those on the other side rather than being told to forget them.

A message from a deceased therapist on the other side explains clearly what happens when someone doesn't address their grief issues. He said, "When someone suffers too long, it pulls them away from work and friends, and interrupts the quality of their relationships." Others eventually gravitate away from self-absorbed depressed people. The person's immune system suffers, and they need to deal with things in a shorter time period so they feel the "shift" toward wellness. They need results quicker, which is what the Repair & Reattachment protocol provides.

This prolonged grief isolates them and affects their interpersonal relationships. They experience a disconnect from life. People who lose someone can experience a deep sense of loss, which is understandable, but therapists can reduce the duration of the suffering. Not treating the grief sets off a ripple effect. It can set people back and prolong suffering, and then a secondary condition sets in which is worse than what they have originally experienced. The Repair & Reattachment grief protocol deals with the grief in a shorter time so the person can experience a shift in perception.

An afterlife connection meditation follows. If you are a group leader, you could use this with your group. If you are doing this alone, read it and then sit quietly and go through the procedure in the meditation to try to have an afterlife connection.

Afterlife Connection Meditation

CREATE a comfortable position for your body, arms unfolded, feet flat on the floor. Close your eyes slowly and take a deep cleansing breath. Breathe in through your nose and out through your mouth. And as you breathe in, imagine the tide coming in and as you exhale through the mouth, the tide going out. So as you begin your breathing, just feel the flow of the waves of the ocean coming in and out. And just begin to feel your body relax. Just letting go. There's nowhere that you need to be right now, no hurry, just let yourself relax as you continue to breathe.

And as you continue to breathe in through your nose, your abdomen goes out. And as you exhale through your mouth, your abdomen gently pulls back to your spine. So continue your breathing and with every exhale just feel your body let go more and more.

Feel your muscles just relaxing. I want you to see the word RELAX written on the inside back of your forehead. And when you see that written on the back of your forehead, let it be a signal to relax from the top of your head all the way down to your feet. Now I would like you to focus on your navel and I want you to go two inches above your navel to the center of gravity and there you will see a round circle. Imagine a light radiating from that circle. And I want you to enter that circle with mind, body and spirit into that round opening, to that deep, deep part of yourself. That all-knowing part. That part where the answers lie, that soft deep, deep part of yourself where love is. Where unconditional love resides. You can call it unconditional love, spirit, higher power, the essence of the source, the God source, whatever fits for you. Be with it. Feel it warm, inviting. And see it in your mind's eye, beginning to expand.

Feel the love for family, friends, pets. Feel the love for those who have passed. And now, float into that part where love is, and rest in it for a while. Relax your body, your mind—no worries no stress, just love. Let go completely. Relaxing. Relax completely.

Now in this love space, see yourself going into even more of a place of unconditional love. Just be with it. And notice it. It may take the form of a garden, flowers, sunshine, an ocean beach, a house or it may just continue to expand to more intense unconditional love. Be open to what comes. In this place you begin to sense people, friends, pets, relatives and those who have passed on. Remember them with love. Imagine you are looking through a picture album.

See the person/pet/others more clearly. See an opening. Step forward into the opening. See more clearly. In this space you may feel a presence, see a face more clearly, be with them right here, right now. Let whatever wants to happen happen while you are bathed in love.

Now step through all the way, through the veil into the afterlife. Experience your deceased loved one: your friend, pet, whoever is there. Be there, and just notice it, without judgment. Be open to this wonderful sacred experience and gift. Feel yourself bathed in love.

Be with them now! Let the love flow freely into your mind, and your whole being. Be in the present moment, be there now. And experience what comes to you. Just notice it!

(Five to ten minute pause.)

I want you to now very slowly begin to do some deep breathing and very slowly come back to the room, knowing you can always step through from this side to the afterlife. The veil is almost transparent. And you will experience the wonderful source where love is. You need only to take time to relax your body, mind and let the stress drain from your body to go to this wonderful place. There you can experience colors, flowers, landscape that is breathtaking and you will be bathed in light and love. It will raise your energy level so that you can connect with loved ones residing in the afterlife.

Slowly take a deep breath through your nose and out through your mouth and very slowly begin to come back to the room, reorienting yourself to time, space and your surroundings.

Biography

Rochelle Wright is a licensed mental health counselor, licensed chemical dependency professional, national certified counselor, EMDR certified therapist for 14 years, and designer of the Repair & Reattachment procedure. She has been a state-licensed grief and trauma psychotherapist for 23 years.

Rochelle developed the Repair & Reattachment procedure that uses bilateral stimulation to enable people to have afterlife connections while in a psychotherapist's office. The Repair & Reattachment method is a psychotherapy procedure that can be administered only by a seasoned, state-licensed psychotherapist. It is a cutting-edge therapy method that does more than simply connect the client with loved ones in the afterlife; it heals grief and trauma in as little as one session.

For information about having a Repair & Reattachment session or being trained to administer the procedure, visit Rochelle's website at RochelleWright.com.

Pioneering Soul Phone Communications

Gary E. Schwartz, Ph.D.

Abstract

    Scientific evidence for the probable existence of a greater spiritual reality - including life beyond death - is expanding rapidly. Moreover, current research strongly indicates the reality of the technological evolution from the cell phone, through the smart phone, to what Schwartz (2011, in his book THE SACRED PROMISE) calls the "soul phone." In this presentation, Schwartz presents both the scientific evidence and careful reasoning that leads him to the provocative conclusion that the probability of humanity developing a soul phone, realistically in the next few years, is the same probability that the light from distant stars has a "kind of immortality." Included in his presentation is a review of his latest published research documenting how the use of highly sensitive and accurate photon detectors (e.g. state-of-the-art silicon photomultiplier and super low light CCD camera systems) can be empirically used to detect the energy and presence of spirit. If the soul phone predication proves to be true, profound societal transformations likely to occur include law (e.g. victims who have been murdered testifying at trials; intellectual property rights of the "deceased"; continued oversight of personal estates and businesses from "the other side"), medicine (e.g. end of physical life care and right to "die" painlessly), and global sustainability (e.g. population control). Potential abuse is also discussed.

Pioneering Soul Phone Communications

Gary E. Schwartz, Ph.D.

Laboratory for Advances in Consciousness and Health
The University of Arizona

Imagination is more important than knowledge.
Albert Einstein

Introduction

This presentation is based in part on my new book, in progress, titled *The Soul Phone Revolution: Understanding the Greatest Transformation in Human History.* The text below is taken from a draft of the Introductory Chapter for this book.

Details concerning some of our methods and findings are presented in my chapter titled "The Soul Phone" in the book *Afterlife Connections* (Hogan, 2014).

Imagining the sPhone

You are about to participate in one of Einstein's favorite activities: the performing of *Gedankenexperiments*—personal thought experiments.

Let's imagine that electronic technology has been created which makes it possible for us (in the physical) to accurately and reliably communicate with people who have physically died (in spirit).

You can think of this technology evolution as the progression from the cell phone, through the smart phone, to what I call the soul phone—or "sPhone" for short.

However, before we embark on our revolutionary soul phone journey and apply the sPhone to personal situations of seminal significance to humanity, we should take a moment for me to explain a heuristic procedure for distinguishing between "us" and "Them" in this book.

"You" and "Me" — "Us" and "Them"

For the sake of clarity of communication, when I refer to "us" (in the physical) I will use small letters, and when I refer to "Those" who have "crossed over" (in spirit) I will capitalize the first letter of the words.

Hence the words "us" and "you" will typically *not* be capitalized, except (of course) when such words are used to start a sentence. For example, I could write the following sentence:

"You will likely be challenged by implications of the soul phone for your life."

The first word "You" is capitalized because it begins the sentence; the word "your" is not because it is within the sentence, and you are physically alive.

By comparison, the words "Them" and "They" will be capitalized when I am specifically speaking about souls (or spirits) "on the other side." Therefore, I will capitalize "Them" and "They" in the middle and end of sentences when I am are specifically referring to "Those" in spirit. For example, I could write the following sentence:

"They will also likely be challenged by the implications of the soul phone for Them."

The first word "They" is capitalized because it begins the sentence; the word "Them" is also capitalized even though it is at the end of the sentence because "They" are in spirit.

Are you ready for "Them"? Here we go.

Trying the Soul Phone

Using this consistent clarification strategy for linguistically distinguishing between us and Them, let's try to imagine that you have ready access to this state-of-the-art soul phone technology and you choose to use it to call your "deceased" family members. What this means is that you can continue to communicate with Them just as you did when They were in the physical. You may choose to regularly call your grandfather and continue your relationship with Him, or call your daughter and continue your relationship with Her.

Please note—I will sometimes put words like "crossed over" and "deceased" in quotes to remind us that these words are metaphors. If the soul phone hypothesis turns out to be valid as predicted, such words will become antiquated since they are erroneous descriptions of the true nature of reality.

Now, let's further imagine that if They wish, They can choose to use the sPhone to *text* you, and you in turn can choose to text Them, whenever They and/or you desire.

And let's imagine that just as you have the freedom to screen your phone calls and text messages and choose who you will respond to (or not), They have this same freedom of choice to respond to you (or not).

Are you ready to consider something a bit more challenging?

Let's try to imagine that you can employ the sPhone not only to call your loved ones and friends, but you can choose to call or text very famous people you might wish to connect with, be they

- visionary Ph.D. scientists like Sir James Clerk Maxwell or Albert Einstein,
- compassionate spiritual leaders like Reverend Martin Luther King or Mother Teresa,
- inspirational political leaders like Presidents Abraham Lincoln or John F. Kennedy, and
- controversial celebrities like the King of Magic, Harry Houdini, or the King of Pop, Michael Jackson.

And let's imagine that if These People choose to, They can accept your sPhone calls or text messages and They can give you the information you desire.

The profound question arises, what implications will this revolutionary technology have for future life on this planet as we—and They—know it?

To help you grasp the profundity of this question, I am about to introduce you to three simple yet visionary transformations that humanity will have to face if the sPhone is successfully developed as predicted.

I should warn you—please be prepared. These "what if" scenarios are extremely novel, deeply challenging, and are highly emotional.

Do Spirits Have Any Intellectual Property (and Associated Financial) Rights?

Let's imagine that Einstein and a team of scientists in spirit have derived a technology for harnessing the energy of the sun in an innovative and cost effective manner which produces virtually no carbon emissions (and hence can greatly reduce manmade carbon dioxide in the atmosphere).

Using the texting capacity of the sPhone, They decide to submit a patent on Their technology, and They do so with the assistance of a skilled patent attorney.

Note that if I had been referring to a "deceased" patent attorney, I would have capitalized Patent Attorney.

The question arises, should They be allowed to receive a US patent on their invention?

In other words, do patent rights and associated intellectual property rights extend to spirit inventors?

What do you think?

To give this visionary exercise greater seriousness—and the Spirits a bit more respect—we can describe the Spirit users of the sPhones as "sPersons."

Moreover, let's imagine not only that Einstein and his Partner's solar energy technology works exactly as claimed, but that the patent is actually granted. Should these sPersons be allowed to (1) determine how Their technology is commercialized—for example, to insure that it will be used wisely and for the greatest good, and (2) should They be given license fees for the technology which They will have the freedom to use as They see fit?

For example, we can imagine that these sPersons might decide, if They wished, to send their grandkids to college, support health programs for the less fortunate, or fund ecology programs.

And of course, we can imagine that They would pay income tax just like anyone else on the license fees they earned, and thereby help to reduce the federal deficit as well as support essential services of government.

In sum, should ownership and income be limited to when a person has a body? Or should ownership and income be granted whenever any "soul"—whether she or he is in body or not—makes a meaningful contribution to humanity and the planet?

What do you think?

Do Spirits Have the Right to Testify at Their Own Trials?

Let's imagine that a seventeen year old unarmed African American boy is walking home after having purchased some candy, and a twenty-nine year old Hispanic man legally carrying a hand gun thinks the boy might be a criminal. A fight ensues, and the boy is tragically shot and killed.

The State Attorney General decides to prosecute the adult male on the charge of second-degree murder. The Defense believes otherwise, and presents their case for self-defense.

In this case, key testimony turns out to be contradictory. For example, the recorded screams of one of the persons in the fight is believed by the boy's parents to be that of their son who was killed, and it is equally believed by the accused parents to be the voice of their adult son who shot the boy.

Let's further imagine that the accused chooses to execute his 5th amendment right not to testify at the trial. Meanwhile, at least one of the witnesses who had been called to testify is allowed to do so via Skype (a practice now allowed under certain conditions).

The question arises, given our imagined existence of a working sPhone and its capacity for sPeople to use it to Skype from "There" to here, should the Boy who was killed have the right to testify at His trial and give His side of the story?

What do you think?

If He is allowed to testify, should the jury be instructed to treat His testimony like any other testimony and use their responsible discernment to determine if this Boy is telling the truth?

Moreover, if the accused was then determined to be guilty by the jury—please note, we are not assuming either actual innocence or guilt here, we are only imagining for the sake of argument that the jury in this instance reached a guilty verdict—and there was a sentencing phase to this trial, should the Boy be allowed to testify as to his thoughts and feelings concerning what would be a just and fair punishment for the man who killed him?

And to make this legal conundrum even more challenging, let's imagine that one or more sPersons would like to donate Their abilities and serve on future juries? The thorny question arises, should sPersons have the right to be considered for possible jury duty?

As you know, trials can sometimes require substantial time and energy on the part of jurors. The voluntary service of sPersons could be argued to have substantial value in terms of reducing personal sacrifices as well as financial losses for jurors.

What do you think?

Do People have the Right to Transition Themselves with the Assistance of Trained Professionals?

Again, remember that we are imagining that the sPhone has been developed and is being extensively used worldwide, just like our contemporary iPhone or Android smart phones are being used today.

Let's imagine a retired couple in their mid-sixties, who have been happily married for forty years. They have two grown children and three adorable grandchildren. The husband unexpectedly has a stroke and "dies."

The wife chooses to continue her relationship with her transitioned Husband via daily sPhone Skype calls plus assorted playful text messages.

Now, depending upon her religious upbringing, she might refer to the place where her husband now resided as being "in the afterlife," "on the other side," or "in heaven." However, in the spirit of our use of more neutral terms sPhone and sPerson, we could simply say that her sPerson husband was now living in "sSpace."

The wife subsequently contracts terminal cancer which is extremely painful. She is bedridden, has severe dizziness, and other cognitive impairments. Not only is she suffering physically and emotionally, but it is costing her estate substantial sums for medical treatment and care.

The combination of (1) her severe pain and suffering, (2) the predicted financial loss to her estate whose assets she and her husband want to go primarily to their children and grandchildren, and secondarily to charities dedicated to children and animal welfare, and (3) her great desire to be with her Husband in sSpace, she makes the carefully reasoned choice to end her physical life now.

The question arises, in light of hypothesized reality of the sPhone and the corresponding definitive evidence of continued life after physical death in sSpace, should she have the right to be able to "kill herself" under these conditions and employ an educated and licensed professional to "transition her" with love and dignity?

Moreover, should society allow the creation of a new specialty of "compassionate transition providers" (CTPs) who are trained to humanely help people complete their physical time on the Earth and transform into "post-physical" beings?

What do you think?

How Well Can You Imagine These Transformative Possibilities?

How effortless (or challenging) it is for you to envision the predicted existence of the sPhone and to imagine the three innovative and emotional implications posed above partly depends upon your current beliefs about the reality (or impossibility) of life after death, as well as your creative ability and conceptual skills in using your imagination.

On the one hand, if you happen to believe in the reality of life after death, and that our energy and information—including our consciousness, personality, and memories—continue after we physically die, then it should not be too much of a stretch for you to envision the emerging reality of the sPhone.

On the other hand, if you strongly believe that when we die it is "ashes to ashes, dust to dust," case closed—*and this is what I was brought up to believe and accept by my parents as well as by my professional training in mainstream science*—then it may be intellectually and emotionally challenging for you to even "entertain the possibility" of the scientific development of an sPhone.

However, whether the idea of the existence of the sPhone is relatively easy—or extremely difficult—for you to personally believe and imagine, this is *not* the critical question here. This book is *not* based upon, nor dependent upon, your ability to imagine my prediction of the emerging reality of the sPhone. This book is carefully designed to help you imagine these possibilities—even if you are a committed skeptic.

The deep question posed in this book is "if" the sPhone does come in existence—and this happens to be the firm conclusion I have reached after almost two decades of extensive scientific research—then *how will our individual and collective lives change*?

Stated somewhat more academically, if research concerning contemporary "immortality science" does prove to be factually true beyond any reasonable doubt in the future, how will our lives change personally, socially, and globally?

The subtitle of my book "Understanding the Greatest Transformation in Human History" is not an exaggeration. If anything, this subtitle is an understatement.

The coming revolution heralded by these scientific discoveries will make previous scientific revolutions seem childlike in comparison. The coming transformation from Materialism to Post-Materialism is truly historic in its scope and significance for science and society.

Virtually every aspect of what it means to be human and how we live on this planet—in terms of our rights and responsibilities—will be directly or indirectly altered by the scientific discovery of the existence of the "immortal soul" and the creation of the sPhone. The title of this book, *The Soul Phone Revolution,* was chosen to convey this profound vision and transformation.

This book was written to awaken you to this coming global paradigm change, and it deserves your careful study. Though I have tried to write it in clear and, occasionally, entertaining fashion, my number one intention is to give you sufficient logic and evidence so you can not only (1) come to your own conclusions about the reality of life beyond death, but also so you can (2) comprehend the sweeping changes that will take place as humanity wakes up to this emerging truth and considers the extraordinary implications of its existence for everything—both physical and post-physical.

To help you see the "big picture" of *The Soul Phone Revolution,* I have written a brief overview of the book on the following page.

Overview to the *Soul Phone Revolution*

Part I of this book is titled "Scientific Reasons to Believe." My purpose here is to provide you with enough convincing laboratory evidence, as well as real life evidence, so you can understand why—and also how—I have come to the conclusion that is it is "Almost Certainly True" that some version of an sPhone will become commercially available in the foreseeable future, and that human rights (both "here" and "There") will transform accordingly.

The words "Almost Certainly True" have been carefully chosen, partly for their precise meaning, and also because they create the playful (and meaningful) acronym ACT. What I am proposing is that it is time for us to ACT to take this coming transformation seriously so we can best prepare for it.

Part I has six chapters.

Chapter 1 provides a brief introduction to five essential criteria I personally employ for responsibly believing in anything. Though this chapter has been written primarily for skeptics, I encourage all readers, including agnostics and believers, to read it closely.

Because the idea of a soul phone is so controversial, it is imperative that you come to understand the set of specific criteria I employ which together lead inexorably to the conclusion that it is time for us (and Them) to take the soul phone revolution seriously and ACT accordingly.

The five essential criteria are:
1. Reason and Theory
2. Scientific Evidence
3. Community of Credible and Trustworthy Believers
4. Direct Personal Experience
5. Responsible Consideration of Skepticism about Criteria 1-4

These five essential criteria are displayed graphically in Figure 1 (shown on the next page).

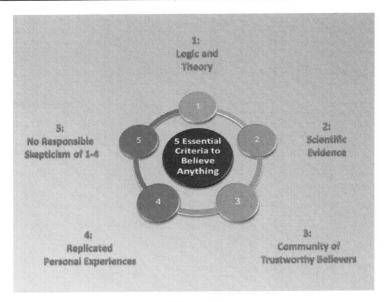

Figure 1

Chapters 2-6 address each of these five criteria as applied to the "soul hypothesis" and the emerging soul phone. By the time you have finished Part I, you will understand why Part II is completely justified.

Part II of this book is titled "Ethical Reasons to be Brave." My purpose here is to illustrate some of the major transformations humanity will face once the soul phone becomes available. Though I have strong opinions about some of the implications of the sPhone, my intent is to raise questions so that you can come to your own conclusions about these anticipated transformations.

Because these transformations are so challenging—and they evoke such powerful feelings both pro and con about the predicted changes—I label them as revolutions. Chapters 7-11 address five areas of revolution:

1. Revolution in Life Planning and Long Term Values
2. Revolution in Intellectual Property and Estates
3. Revolution in Health Care and the Dying Process
4. Revolution in Education, Business, and Religion
5. Revolution of Sustainability and Global Population

By the time you have finished Part II, you will understand why I had to write this book, and write it now.

The Conclusion and Appendices at the end of the book provide additional discussion about (1) love, immortality science and the soul, (2) how to apply the five essential criteria for believing anything, and (3) how to prevent the potential misuse of the technology.

Understanding Why the Soul Phone Revolution Is Vitally Important—The Bottom Line is Love

Before we address in Part I the five essential criteria for responsibly believing that something is true, and you learn how to apply the five criteria systematically to the emergence of soul communication technology, it is valuable for us to remember some practical and personal reasons for our taking time out of our busy lives to ponder the soul phone revolution.

The bottom line to this work is love.

Consider the following potential reasons for caring about the soul phone revolution:

- If you have known anyone you deeply loved who has "died," and you would love to be able to continue your relationship with Her or Him, **AND/OR**

- You would love to be able to gain advice and counsel from specific Persons "on the other side" to help you in your professional and personal life, **AND/OR**

- If you are anticipating that you will be "dying" in the future, and you would love to be able to continue your loving relationships with specific family members and friends on the Earth after you transition, **AND/OR**

- You would love to be able to look forward to continuing to be of service to humanity and the Earth after you have "crossed over," and you want to prepare for this higher purpose while you are still here in the physical, **THEN**

- *It is prudent that you spend some of your time now envisioning the potential emergence of the soul phone and its vast implications for you, your loved ones, and society as a whole.*

If any potential technological breakthrough has the power to celebrate and advance love and caring—both here and "There"—this is it. If ever was a time for us to be brave, it is now.

As a well-known agent in Hollywood recently put it after hearing about the ongoing soul phone research, he said (and I paraphrase slightly):

"This work makes me feel like Jimmy Stewart in 'It's a Wonderful Life.'"

And as a guest at Canyon Ranch recently put it after hearing my lecture titled *The Sacred Promise: How Science is Discovering Spirits Collaboration with Us in Our Daily Lives,* he said (and I paraphrase slightly):

"This work nourishes the kindness of our Spirit, and it is good news."

The question is whether we are imaginative enough and brave enough to face these spectacular challenges and opportunities. I end this overview with a stanza from the song *Brave* written by Josh Groban and colleagues. I invite all of us to savor their inspirational message, which I have expanded from "you" to "we":

> We wanna run away run away and we say that it can't be so
> We wanna look away look away
> But we stay 'cause it's all so close
> When we stand up and hold out our hands
> In the face of what we don't understand
> Our reason to be brave....

Bibliography

Hogan, R.C. (Ed.). (2014). *Afterlife Connections: 16 Proven Methods, 85 True Accounts.* Normal, IL: Greater Reality Publications.

Biography

Gary E. Schwartz, Ph.D., is Professor of Psychology, Medicine, Neurology, Psychiatry, and Surgery at the University of Arizona and director of the Laboratory for Advances in Consciousness and Health. He is also Corporate Director of Development of Energy Healing at Canyon Ranch. Gary received his Ph.D. in psychology from Harvard University in 1971 and was an assistant professor at Harvard for five years. He later served as a professor of psychology and psychiatry at Yale University, director of the Yale Psychophysiology Center, and co-director of the Yale Behavioral Medicine Clinic, before moving to Arizona in 1988. He has published more than four hundred and fifty scientific papers, including six papers in the journal *Science*. Gary has also co-edited eleven academic books, is the author of *The Energy Healing Experiments* (2007), *The G.O.D. Experiments* (2006), *The Afterlife Experiments* (2002), *The Truth about Medium* (2005), and *The Living Energy Universe* (1999). His latest book *The Sacred Promise: How Science is Discovering Spirit's Collaboration with Us in Our Daily Lives* was published in 2011. Gary is highly experienced in speaking publicly about health psychology, energy healing, and spiritual research. He has been interviewed on major network television shows including *Dateline* and *Good Morning America,* as well as on *MSNBC, Nightline, Anderson Cooper 360,* and *The O'Reilly Factor.* His work has been the subject of documentaries and profiles on *Discovery, HBO, Arts & Entertainment, Fox* and the *SciFi Channel,* among others. His research on mediumship and spirit communication is featured in the 2013 document *The Life After Death Project.*

Retrieval: Being of Service Here and There

Bruce Moen

Abstract

    In one of my earliest memories from childhood, I remember looking at the world surrounding me as a five-year-old and asking three questions: Where was I before it was here? What am I supposed to do while I'm here? Where will I go when I leave here? My life has been guided by my curiosity seeking answers to those three questions.

    By somewhere in my mid-20s, I'd satisfied my curiosity about some of the places I have been before this lifetime, and so I turned to my second question. After struggling with the question for far too long I realized no one in their 20s is equipped to even ask that question much last find many answers. Somewhere in my late 20s I began to focus on that third question: Where will I go when I leave here?

    From many of the books I read during my search, I had concluded that if our afterlife existed it would be found in the same neighborhood as we go during dreaming. When I discovered lucid dreaming, I began trying to learn that technique to see if I could explore the dreaming neighborhood using it. Lucid dreaming is a form of dreaming in which we are aware that we are dreaming, and therefore have some conscious control of your activities during the lucid dream. While attempting to learn how to do lucid dreaming one of those lucid dreams led to the discovery of Robert Monroe's first book, "Journeys Out of the Body." Monroe's accounts of his out-of-body experiences described a technique that I judged to be superior to lucid dreaming for my afterlife exploration experiences. And so I began a several-years-long-attempt to learn that technique, an unsuccessful attempt I might add! In all

83

*the years I pursued that goal I succeeded perhaps five or ten
times. Those successes always occurred unexpectedly and at
least two thirds of them lasted no more than a few seconds. Only
one of these experiences was of long enough duration for me to
discover that verifiable physical world information could be
gathered using the out-of-body technique. With feathers from my
"one white crow" in hand I continue trying to master the
technique, eventually attending Monroe's Institute in Faber,
Virginia in 1991.*

*I did not make any progress at The Monroe Institute in my
quest to master the out-of-body experience technique, but I did
discover they were teaching a form of afterlife exploration in a
new six-day program called Lifeline. After attending the Lifeline
program several times, it took me another 3 1/2 years of using
those techniques to convince myself that the afterlife does
actually exist. I highly recommend the Monroe Institute and its
programs to anyone desiring to discover whether or not we are
indeed more than our physical bodies.*

Retrieval: Being of Service Here and There

by Bruce Moen

Since my own perceptual skill development and evidence gathering
was for the most part a direct result of attending The Monroe Institute's
six-day Lifeline program, some of the elements of that program were
used in the development of my system. Specifically, the concept of
"retrieval" is used as a vehicle for making contact and interacting with
those who have died. The Monroe Institute's Lifeline program is billed
as a program of Service Here and There. Service Here describes a
process in which the information gathered through contact and
communication with a known deceased person is related to a physically
living friend, relative or loved one of the deceased person. Service Here
can act as a catalyst to aid the healing of grief on the part of the
physically living, as well as heal unresolved issues between a physically
living person and the deceased person. Service There describes a process
in which program graduates perform what is called "retrieval."

Retrieval in the Monroe Institute's Lifeline context assumes (from
Robert Monroe's direct experience) that when people die some of them
get "stuck" before reaching a more appropriate place for them to exist
beyond physical reality. While many of the various reasons people get
stuck after death are not fully understood, my system makes the same

assumption. It also assumes, as does Lifeline, that certain interactions between a physically living human and the stuck, deceased individual can more quickly resolve whatever issues are causing the person to be stuck. And that once these issues are resolved, the stuck person can easily be assisted in moving to a more appropriate place to exist within our afterlife. Retrieval thus serves as a vehicle for exploration, and our afterlife as a testing ground in which potentially verifiable information can be gathered from the deceased person.

By my early 40s, I'd gathered enough verifiable information using my Lifeline training to convince myself of our afterlife's existence. I'd gathered a considerable body of knowledge and understanding about what our human existence is like beyond physical death. Curiosity about my third childhood question, "Where will I go when I leave here," was satisfied. It was then that I began to discovering answers to my second question: "What am I supposed to do while I'm here?"

Through the years as my curiosity guided me to answers to these questions, I came to realize that there are many of us humans seeking answers to those same three questions. And in my opinion, of those three the one that has the greatest potential impact on one's life in a positive way is a direct knowledge of the existence of our afterlife. As the years go by for all of us, many begin focusing more on wanting to know what happens after we die.

Some of us who've lost loved ones worry about where our loved ones have gone, if they still exist at all. But, for the vast majority of us, answers to resolve those questions and those worries appear to be both unknown and unknowable. No matter what we have been taught to believe, or have read or heard, there is always room to doubt someone else's experience. In my own voyages of perception beyond physical reality I discovered that truly satisfying answers to these questions can never come from any other source than one's own direct experience or beliefs. Though both science and religion attempt to provide answers to these questions for people through their beliefs and rationale, their answers will always leave room for doubt.

While struggling to find those answers for myself I learned a lot about what works and what doesn't. In my late 40s I began to feel a strong desire to find a way to help others do what I had done. Knowing that I will continue to exist beyond my physical death had profound effects upon my life and the lives of those around me. I wanted to find a way that others could experience this firsthand. And so I began developing a simple system of concepts, techniques and exercises based on my own experience. The goal I set for myself was that almost anyone would be able to use this system to find answers to these questions through their own direct experience. And, that this system requires nothing more on the part of workshop participants than being open-minded to the possibility of our afterlife's existence. This system does not require that a person have any special psychic gifts or talents, nor does it require learning complicated, difficult techniques such as lucid dreaming or out-of-body experience. It does not require the participant to take on any of my beliefs. There are no special diets, magic potions, etc. Instead, it is a set of simple, small steps that facilitate greatly accelerated development of the necessary perceptual and navigational skills to explore the supposed existence of our afterlife. I've been teaching this system since 1999 in workshops around the world and the results demonstrate it successfully satisfies my goals.

Core Assumption

The foundational core of this system is the concept that "big C" Consciousness exists as a single entity that is a unified, coherent, interconnected integration of all of forms of known and unknown "little c" consciousnesses. And, that all forms of "little c" consciousness are accessible by all other forms of "little c" consciousness.

The core assumption implies that exploration of any area within "big C" Consciousness, such as our afterlife, is accomplished by simply shifting our focus of attention, or awareness, into that area of Consciousness, and then using our "nonphysical senses" to become aware of and interact with others that may exist within that area of Consciousness. The system of concepts, techniques and exercises that I teach accomplishes exploration of our afterlife in exactly that manner. One learns how to shift one's focus of attention into the area of Consciousness we call the afterlife, and then using one's nonphysical senses to become aware of and interact with those who exist within that afterlife.

Imagination as a Means of Perception

The key concept used to explore our afterlife area of consciousness is to use imagination as a means of perception. According to the Oxford English dictionary the word "imagination" is defined as "the faculty or action of forming new ideas, or images or concepts of external objects not present to the senses."

One of the difficulties for the student of my system is the common confusion regarding the words "fantasy" and "imagination." Typically when someone says, "It only happened in my imagination," what they mean is, "it is only a fantasy." I would say to that person, "Of course it happened in only your imagination; it is the sense we use to perceive our fantasies, but it can also be used to perceive things that are real. The question then becomes: How do we know whether what we are perceiving is a fantasy or something real? The short answer is that we cannot tell whether we are perceiving fantasy or reality *during our exploration experiences*. We can only discover that after the experience is completed. What I call "The Basic Premise" is used to make that determination.

The Basic Premise

The Basic Premise provides a conceptual basis one uses to judge the reality, or non-reality, of awareness and interaction with others during exploration of these experiences. That Basic Premise is:

1. Find any way to contact and communicate with a person who is known to be deceased.

2. Gather information from that person that there is absolutely no way for you to know except by that contact and communication with that deceased person.

3. Seek to validate and verify that this information is accurate, true and real.

4. If the information can be verified as real you may not have proven anything yet, but you've gathered some evidence this person continues to exist, somewhere.

5. Repeat this process until the weight of your own evidence, gathered through your own direct experience, leads you to your own conclusions regarding the existence of our human afterlife.

Grandpa was a Bank Robber

A short story will illustrate how this is done.

Suppose I wanted to visit with my paternal grandfather, a man who died two years before I was born. Using imagination as a means perception for contact and communication with him, I might begin by fantasizing or pretending a conversation with him. I could begin by imagining a scene in which this contact takes place. I could pretend I'm sitting on the back porch of a house, looking over an unkempt yard with tall grass and weeds. I imagine it's a hot, muggy summer day with puffy little white clouds drifting along with the wind in a deep blue sky. I might imagine the sound of leaves of a tree rustling in a light breeze. Since nothing is better on a hot, muggy summer day than an ice-cold beer, I might pretend I'm holding two bottles of ice-cold Green Belt beer.

I imagine I hear my grandfather's footsteps in the house behind me. I pretend to call out to him, "Hey Gramps, come on out back, I've got something for you." I imagine the sound of an old creaky screen door opening, his footsteps approaching, and an old man sitting down next to me. After pretending to hand him one of the beers I begin a fantasy conversation with old man.

"Gramps, my name is Bruce."

"Yeah, I know," I pretend he says.

"I was born, two years after you died," I tell him.

"Yeah, I know," I pretend he replies.

I'm kind of bad at this fantasizing a conversation thing, but I continue until the conversation takes an unexpected turn. Out of the blue, Gramps leans close to me and says, "You know, when I was a younger man I was a bank robber!"

Now, I'm pretty sure I made that up, but these unexpected events often lead to verifiable information. So, I play along with Gramps to see where this takes the experience.

"What's the last bank you robbed?" I ask.

"First National Bank of Eau Claire, Wisconsin; got away with $12,000," he replies.

"What did you do with the money?" I ask.

"Put it in an old metal fishing tackle box and buried it ten paces north of the oak tree in the backyard of the house on Elm Street," he says.

"Did you ever get to spend that money?" I ask.

"That wasn't the first bank I robbed, Bruce. The cops pinched me two weeks later and sent me to Stillwater Prison. Hell, kid, I died in that prison!"

As I'm scrambling to come up with my next question I see another old man walking toward me across the backyard. I pretend to offer this man a beer and ask him, "Who are you?"

"I'm Arne Svenson," he says, "I was your Grandpa's cellmate in Stillwater Prison. I was there with him when he died."

I continue in this imaginary conversation. Sometimes I struggle to make it up, sometimes something unexpected happens and I play along to gather as much information as I can. When I finish with this experience I make detailed, written notes documenting everything I can remember. Then I give some thought to how I might go about attempting to verify the information I gathered. If my father was still alive (my deceased grandfather's son), I could call him. After exchanging in a little small talk I might ask, "Dad, is it is true that grandpa was a bank robber?"

Knowing my dad his gruff response might be, "Who told you?" "That's a family secret that no one is supposed to talk about."

"Nobody told me, Dad," I reply.

"Tell me who it was!" my dad would ask more forcefully.

"Dad, it was more like I had a dream Grandpa was in and he told me," I reply.

"Cut the crap, Bruce, who told you?" He insists.

"Dad, Dad, no one told me, honest. Dad, did your father die in prison?" I ask.

His voice relaxing a little, he answers, "Yes."

"Did you ever live in a house on Elm Street?" I ask.

"Yeah, we were living there when the cops arrested my dad."

"Was there a big oak tree in the backyard?"

"Yeah, I had a swing in that tree when I was a kid," he replies.

"Do you know if that house is still standing?"

"Yes, it's still there. I drive by it sometimes, and remember those times," he says.

Remembering the money, I say, "Dad, get your shovel. I'm coming over to pick you up and we're gonna take a little ride."

If we go to that house and convince the owners to let us dig a hole in the back yard, ten paces north of the stump of a big oak tree . . . If we find a metal tackle box with a bag labeled, First National Bank of Eau Claire with about twelve thousand dollars in it . . . It doesn't really prove anything, but it's pretty good evidence that what started as a fantasy conversation with a dead man resulted in verifiably real information.

That story, a fantasy I might add, illustrates how imagination can be used as a means of perception in exploration of the afterlife. This next story is not a fantasy. It's the actual experience of a workshop participant using imagination to make contact with a known deceased person. I'd like to share the participant's experience here to give you the flavor of what's possible. This example is in my view one of many spectacularly successful completions of the Basic Premise. I call it the "You can get in your car now" experience of "Jacquom."

You Can Get in Your Car Now

A workshop in Germany was attended by approximately 30 participants, about half of whom were psychotherapists. They were debriefing the exercise called Getting a Special Message. In this exercise each of the 30 participants writes, on small, identical slips of paper, the name of a person they personally know who's deceased. These slips of paper are then folded twice and placed in a basket. Then, one by one, each participant draws one of the slips of paper from the basket. Each participant now has in his or her possession a slip of paper with the name of the person known to be deceased. Since the slips of paper are all identical and chosen at random, they have no way of knowing whom this deceased person is, nor do they know which of their fellow participants provided that name. Once all the slips of paper have been drawn the exercise begins.

The exercise is similar to a guided meditation. Participants are seated in chairs with their eyes closed and are following my verbal instruction. After following instructions intended to help participants relax and a few other instructions, they are ready to begin the guided imagery portion of the exercise. This guided imagery portion might be an imaginary walk in a forest, a walk along the beach, or some other imaginary journey intended to stimulate their imagination for use as a means of perception in the exercise. Then, the exercise to make contact and communicate with the deceased person, whose name they've randomly drawn, begins.

My instructions guide participants into an imaginary meeting with the deceased person. During this meeting participants are asked to gather certain information from that person. This information includes things like the person's physical appearance, manner of dress, age, manner of death, habits, basic personality and several other such details. The deceased person is asked to show, or tell about, a physical lifetime scene he or she was in, together with the participant who wrote their name on the slip of paper, that both would remember. The deceased person is also asked to show, tell or give something as proof that this contact and communication with them is real.

Near the end of the exercise, the deceased person is asked for a special, meaningful message to be given to the person who provided their name. After the completion of the exercise and making very detailed written notes of their experience during the exercise, one by one each participant shares that experience with the entire group. The name of the deceased person is not disclosed to the group until all the information is shared. The participant who provided that name then identifies himself or herself and gives feedback regarding the accuracy of the information that is just been shared.

Until this exercise in the German workshop, Jacquom, one of the participants who is a psychotherapist, had learned the process of retrieval. He saw these experiences as nothing more than flights of fantasy driven by his own imagination, and therefore completely and totally fabricated. Nevertheless, Jacquom had played along with the previous experiences to learn the process of retrieval.

During the debriefing of this exercise at that workshop in Germany, Jacquom prefaced his sharing the details of his experience with what I found to be a rather odd statement. Jacquom was one of the psychotherapists in the group who felt that what I was teaching led people to believe that the fantasy stories they were making up during the exercises are real experiences. In his prefacing statement before describing his experience, Jacquom said, "If any of the information I received during this exercise is verified I'm going to get up from my chair, go out to my car, drive myself to the nearest psychiatric facility, and check myself in."

After sharing some mundane details like age, manner of dress, manner of death, and so on, Jacquom shared the physical lifetime scene that both the deceased and the person who provided his name were in together and would both remember. In that scene Jacquom saw a small round table crowded with cigarette-butt-filled ashtrays, several empty coffee cups, and a chessboard. He said it felt like a small sidewalk café in a city on the southern coast France. There were two men sitting on opposite sides of the table casually chatting and playing chess.

In response to Jacquom's asking the deceased to show him, tell him, or give him something as proof that this contact and communication is real, the deceased man said that he and the man who had provided his name often played chess. And, that before his death, the deceased man had given the participant a chess set as a gift. The deceased man also said that one of the white knights in this chess set had one of his ears broken off.

It was at this point that one of the other participants, Richard, spoke. Richard's first words were, "You can get in your car now." Richard continued by saying every piece of the mundane detail information Jacquom had given were accurate and correct. Richard explained that his friend had died a couple of years earlier. He remembered the specific sidewalk café scene in which he and his friend were playing chess. He also disclosed that his friend had indeed given him a chess set as a gift before he died, and that indeed one of the white knights was missing one of its ears. Jacquom immediately became so disoriented and befuddled that he could not share any more of his experience, so we never did get to hear the deceased man's special message for Richard. The level of verification in Jacquom's experience during the workshop is more common than most people would expect.

So, How Does This Happen?

Assuming that all areas of Consciousness, including the ones we call physical reality and the afterlife, are fully integrated and interconnected as a single Consciousness, Jacquom's experience requires the development of only three basic skills: navigation to and from various areas of consciousness; perception of one's surrounding environment within these areas of Consciousness; and communication with others who exist within that environment.

Navigation

Of these three skills navigation between the physical world reality and human afterlife consciousness is the simplest. Workshop participants are taught to rely on people called Helpers to provide navigation to and from various areas of Consciousness. Conceptually, Helpers provide the same services as a scout or guide assisting explorers in unknown territories. They are viewed as nonphysical beings who reside within nonphysical realities. Others might call these Helpers "Angels," "Guides," "Spirits," "Spirit Guides," or some similar term. I prefer the term Helper as it avoids some of the religious and New Age jargon and baggage. These Helpers know the locations and situations of various deceased individuals and are tasked with guiding the participant to such individuals and providing whatever other assistance the participant requires. All the participant has to do is be willing to imagine following the Helper to the deceased individual.

With sufficient practice, conscious interaction with the Helper for navigation to and from areas of Consciousness becomes less necessary. Participants can navigate on their own by learning to shift their focus of attention from one area of Consciousness to another using their Intent.

Shifting One's Focus of Attention

Workshop participants first learn a simple relaxation exercise. And then begin to practice shifting their focus of attention from one area of consciousness to another in a simple way. While seated in a chair with their eyes closed and relaxed, participants are asked to focus their attention at the bottoms of their feet. To help them understand the concept I explain that if I asked them to tell me what the bottoms of their feet are feeling in this moment they would have to shift their focus of attention to the bottoms of their feet to answer that question. Participants are then asked to shift their focus of attention to the top of the head. We might say they are shifting their focus of attention between the "bottoms of the feet" area of consciousness and the "top of the head" area of consciousness. This is repeated several times and then participants might be asked to shift their focus of attention to the kitchen or bedroom of their home areas of consciousness. After a few more simple exercises participants have their own direct experience from which to learn and understand the concept of shifting their focus of attention from one area of consciousness to another. I then explain to them that conceptually what they've just learned to do is no different than learning to shift their focus of attention into any area of Consciousness, including the one called the afterlife.

Perception Within Nonphysical Realities

In this part of the system that I teach, participants are introduced to the concept of nonphysical senses. If they are going to be able to perceive their surrounding environment within a nonphysical reality, they'll need to use something like their physical senses of sight, hearing, touch, taste and smell, but use them within a nonphysical environment. I feel the best way for me to explain to participants is by way of demonstration. With that in mind I ask all participants who are willing to do so to join in this little exercise. This is the narration I give:

When you are ready and in a comfortable position in your chair to begin the exercise please close your eyes and begin by taking some long, slow, deep relaxing breaths.

Take in one more slow, deep, relaxing breath. Remember one of your parents; just remember one of your parents.

Take in one more slow, deep, relaxing breath. Remember one of your pets; just remember a pet.

Take in one more slow, deep, relaxing breath. Remember a radio and remember listening to a favorite piece of music or a favorite program on the radio.

Take in one more slow, deep, relaxing breath. Remember an orange, the fruit; remember holding an orange in your hand. Remember the feel of the shape and weight of the orange, its color and its texture. Remember peeling the orange, its scent and the feel of it against your lips. Remember eating the orange.

One more slow, deep relaxing breath and then when you are ready please open your eyes.

And the rest of you, please open your eyes.

By a show of hands how many of you would say that when I asked you to remember a parent and a pet during this exercise you saw something in any way? How many would say that you saw something in color? In black and white? Clear and in focus? Fuzzy and indistinct? In motion like a movie or video? More like a still picture?

How many of you who would say they didn't see anything but blackness but would say that you knew which parent or pet you were remembering and what they were doing?

By a show of hands how many of you would say that when I asked you to remember a favorite piece of music or program on the radio during this exercise that you heard something in any way? How many would say what you heard was clear and distinct? What you heard was in a voice different from your own? Coming from outside of you? More like someone else's voice in your mind? More like hearing your own voice in your mind? More like just the thought of what music was playing or what was being said in the favorite program? How many would say you didn't hear anything but you knew what music was being played or what was being said or talked about?

When you remembered the orange how many of you would say you felt its shape or its weight in your hand? Were aware of its texture? Saw its shape or color? Smelled its scent when you peeled the orange? Felt the orange against your lips? Tasted it? Anyone have to deal with the seeds? How many of you had something different from an orange in your experience?

This little exercise is intended to guide you to your own, direct experience of what I call your nonphysical senses. And it points to an important difference between our physical and nonphysical senses. For example our physical sense of sight is a fairly narrow range of experience. Normal physical sight is always: in color; it's normally sharp, clear and in focus; it's in 3D and holographic; it's in motion; it is incapable of perceiving nonphysical things; and, we always assume that what we physically see is real.

When I first began trying to explore nonphysical realities I believed I would see within nonphysical realities in exactly the same way I see physical reality. One of the biggest mistakes I made was to assume that if something didn't look like it would using physical sight it was by definition "not real." I threw away tons of perfectly good potentially verifiable evidence until I began to understand that nonphysical sight is a much broader range of experience. That experience can be understood as existing along a continuum with physical-world-type images on one end, through fuzzy black and white, all the way to being in a room with no doors, no windows and no lights with your eyes closed. All you "see" is blackness but you know what you are looking at and can describe it in detail.

I had to come to understand and accept that the visual quality of images I saw non-physically has absolutely nothing to do with the validity or verifiability of the information that can be gathered from those images. That realization led to greatly accelerated evidence gathering that met the criteria of my Basic Premise. Each of our nonphysical senses shares this characteristic of a much broader range of experience than its physical world senses experience.

Jacquom's "You can get in your car now" experience demonstrates the kind of verifiable evidence gathering that is often accomplished by workshop participants with just a few hours of training in the system I teach. With just an open-minded approach and a willingness to play along, pretend, and fantasize, much can be accomplished in a short time.

People often hear me say that exploring our afterlife is so easy that the hardest thing to do is to believe you are doing it. And the limitation of our perception by our beliefs and expectations is a whole subject all by itself.

There is, of course, much more taught in my workshops than I've been able to describe here. I invite any of you interested to attend one of my workshops. If there are some reading this who might be interested in collaborative research, I am open to talking about that possibility.

Biography

Bruce Moen is an author and international lecturer on exploring the afterlife and performing "retrievals." In a retrieval, someone from this side of life goes to the afterlife to help people who are "stuck" after their passing from the Earth plane and unable or unwilling to go on to the next level of their lives. Bruce's work is based on the Monroe Institute's Lifeline procedure.

Bruce is an engineering consultant with his own firm. You can read more about him on his website at afterlife-knowledge.com.

The Preponderance
of the Evidence

Suzanne Giesemann, M.A.

Abstract

The primary goal of an evidential medium is to validate the continuity of consciousness beyond the death of the physical body. The eternality of the soul cannot yet be proven using our current technology. However, applying the same standards used by our system of justice, we can come as close to proof as possible. Evidential medium Suzanne Giesemann explains how providing the preponderance of evidence can change belief systems, opening minds to a far greater reality. Suzanne shares stunning evidence received from beyond the physical domain which has been validated using scientific methods. She reveals the keys to receiving more evidential communication with the unseen world with the goal of raising the standards and credibility of modern-day mediumship.

The Preponderance of the Evidence

by Suzanne Giesemann

I am Suzanne Giesemann, and I am an evidential medium. If that sounds like a greeting from "AA," that's because a few years ago, when I discovered the ability to communicate with the non-physical realm, I had some difficulty announcing that fact in public. It wasn't that I was ashamed of my new line of work. It was because the work was so drastically different from my first career.

My background includes 20 years as a U.S. Navy officer. I retired with the rank of commander and served at the very highest level of our military organization. I had the honor of serving as a commanding officer and as a special assistant to the chief of naval operations. The greatest

97

honor was being asked by the Chairman of the Joint Chiefs of Staff to be his aide-de-camp. In that capacity I went everywhere he went, from our office at the Pentagon to Capitol Hill and to the White House. I flew on Air Force One with the President and met with kings and queens.

My husband, Ty, spent 26 years in the military, and my step-daughter, Susan, followed in our footsteps, joining the Marines. She reached the rank of sergeant, but was tragically killed in 2008 when she was struck by lightning. It was Susan's death that led me to a medium in search of evidence that the spirit survives the transition we call death. I received such convincing evidence in that reading that I wanted to share the comforting, life-changing messages of mediumship with as wide of an audience as possible.

To achieve this goal I wrote the biography of medium Anne Gehman. This became my Hay House book, *The Priest and the Medium*. It was while researching the life of medium Janet Nohavec for a subsequent biography that I attended Janet's classes on mediumship to learn more about her work. She surprised me by calling me to the front of the classroom and saying, "There's a spirit here that I want you to link into and tell me what you sense." I was even more surprised when I brought through several pieces of verifiable evidence from the deceased father of one of the students in the class.

I finished Janet's biography along with her series of classes on mediumship. The evidence I continued to bring through from the loved ones of my classmates convinced me that I had uncovered an ability I was previously unaware I had. It helped me to overcome my left-brained military upbringing and accept the existence of a reality beyond the five senses.

I decided to study where my mentor Janet had studied. I traveled to Stansted, England, to study with some of the best evidential mediums in the world. I've used the words "evidence" and "evidential" several times already in this presentation. What do I mean by evidence? It's the details that a medium brings through in a reading that they couldn't possibly know—things like, How did the person die? What kind of work did they do? How old were they when they passed? British mediums stress the evidence. This is a real cultural difference, because unfortunately, many American mediums do not.

Why do I say "unfortunately"? Because there is a greater reality, and it is inhabited by intelligent beings who are anxious to communicate with us. The work of a medium can bring incredible comfort to those who are grieving, but when a medium gives messages that lack evidence, they give skeptics of mediumship grounds to denigrate this vital work.

In an editorial in *The Journal for Spiritual and Consciousness Studies* (2014), editor Mike Tymn provided definitions of the four types of skeptics:

> The Seeker understands the difference between evidence and proof while recognizing that absolute proof is rare in any scientific endeavor.
>
> The Shrugger hasn't really examined the evidence for or against paranormal phenomena but simply wants to appear "intelligent" by wearing the skeptic's badge.
>
> The Smirker thinks of him or herself as too mentally gifted or advanced to believe in anything that is not subject to strict scientific "proof" while failing to recognize that few things supposedly proved by science are proved with absolute certainty. The smirker is to science what the fundamentalist is to religion. There is no way his ego will allow him to be wrong.
>
> The Scoffer is the smirker in the extreme. He or she is close-minded and has already made up his or her mind about everything. They have changed the definition of "skeptic" from "one who doubts" to "one who will never accept."

My mentor claims that I was the biggest skeptic she knew. I would agree with that. But happily, I fell into the category of a seeker. What allowed me to move from doubt in the spirit world to knowing beyond any doubt that there is a greater reality is the evidence.

Evidence is quite different from "messages" in a reading. Evidence is information about the deceased person or the client that can be validated and that the medium could not possibly know. Messages are communications for the client that one may or may not be able to validate, and there is no way of proving the source. An example of evidence is, "This gentleman sold shoes for a living." An example of a message is, "This gentleman says it is very peaceful where he is now."

The primary goal of an evidential medium is to validate the continuity of consciousness beyond the death of the physical body. The eternality of the soul cannot yet be proven using our current technology. However, applying the same standards used by our system of justice, we can come as close to proof as possible. Providing the preponderance of evidence can change belief systems, opening minds to a far greater reality.

The challenge is that there are no set standards for this work. Some mediums are satisfied with only giving messages that cannot be validated. This does little to satisfy the many people who need validation.

Many of the clients who come to me want badly to hear from their loved ones, but aren't convinced that mediumship is real. I completely understand that. I very clearly recall one gentleman who sat down and announced, "I'm on the fence about this whole thing." I replied, "That's fine. We'll let the evidence speak for itself."

During his reading I received quite a bit of evidence, including the following that all proved very accurate: his father talked about a special knife he had given his son, and he showed me a bow and arrow as a way of letting me know of his Native American heritage. I told my client that I sensed a child that had been miscarried. He said, "Nobody knows about that!" but I assured him the spirit of that child knew this. I also brought through a friend who called my client "Bro" and showed me that he smoked "funny cigarettes." My client's eyes grew very wide at that bit of evidence! After I brought through a step-brother whom I described as "angry at the world," I asked my client how he felt about mediumship now. His reply was an emphatic, "I can tell you one thing, I'm not on the fence anymore!"

By my way of thinking, the burden of proof rests with the spirits on the other side and the medium working together to move people off the fence. When we do that, the results change lives. Let me zero in on a young man whose name is Noah, who came through in a Skype call reading with his mother.

Without knowing anything about my client, I correctly sensed that she had lost a son who was six or seven years old. I felt a pain in my head and knew intuitively that he had passed from an aneurism that burst. He talked about his "paw paw" and how he enjoyed the cows on his paw paw's farm. She said, yes he did indeed, call his grandpa "paw paw." His mother then asked if he could say something about his brother. Noah then showed me horses. His mother stated that he couldn't have said anything better, because his brother used to help Noah with therapeutic riding.

Based on what he showed me next, I told his mother that Noah must have had a very special ride on a red fire engine because he was showing me himself sitting on top of it. She said, "It's his bed, and I'm sitting on it now." Since this was a Skype call, I could see her only from the waist up. Excited about this wonderful evidence, I said, "Show it to me," and she held her iPad so I could see his bed. His mother said, "You told me to sit somewhere where I would feel peaceful, so I chose Noah's bedroom. In fact, he died in this bed." And thanks to the evidential vision of Noah riding a red fire engine, his mother found great peace from knowing that her son is still very much around her.

I could share evidence like Noah's for every one of the people who have come through in my readings. It's comforting, it's healing, it's revealing, but it is highly anecdotal. We don't know if the things I'm sharing represented 10% of the information that came through in these readings or 90%.

That's why the spirit world sent me to noted afterlife researcher Dr. Gary Schwartz. They wanted me to be able to validate their existence. Why do I say "the spirit world sent me to him?" In February 2012, I was sitting on my couch reading a book by Dr. Schwartz, when I became aware of the presence of a woman in spirit who identified herself to me as Gary's mentor, Susy Smith. I filled two pages with information about Susy and Gary that I had no way of knowing, and I was instructed to send it to Gary. Ever the scientist, Dr. Schwartz put me to the test by having me ask Susy a series of inscrutable questions, such as, "Have Susy tell you about the foxes." The answers I received from her must have convinced this expert researcher of mediums, because he replied, "It appears Susy has chosen you to work with me."

I had the opportunity to do experimental explorations with Dr. Schwartz in his laboratory at the University of Arizona, during which he had me contact seven spirits, each of whom gave me outstanding evidence. Since that time, he has sent me several people for readings and subjected the results to the system of scoring the evidence that he has used for over 15 years.

And so, when the spirit of a young man named Wolf came to me unexpectedly in the pre-dawn hours last July and gave me enough evidence to fill 8 pages in a notebook, I found it interesting when he said, "Have my parents score this, like Gary."

I found this prospect very exciting because I had not yet had any experience with this young man. I was not scheduled to give a reading to his parents until two days later. This visit was unexpected, and best of all from a scientific point of view, it was completely "blind," because I had no feedback as Wolf was giving me the evidence.

Wolf painted himself as a most unusual young man. These were not generic character traits that would match just anyone. In addition to the messages Wolf gave me, his visit included 48 verifiable items, which his parents dutifully scored according to Dr. Schwartz' system. Per his instructions, they also chose a cousin of Wolf's of the same age to serve as a "control" to rule out chance.

Dr. Schwartz summarized this unexpected pre-reading beautifully when he said it was the best of its kind he had seen. That's very affirming, but I prefer the actual statistics.

Dr. Schwartz stated, "The probability of the difference between the scoring for Wolf versus the cousin as being explainable as 'chance' is less than one in a million ($p<.0000001$). By contrast, the required criteria for statistical significance used in psychological research is less than one in twenty ($p<.05$). Hence, the test for the Wolf versus cousin data is statistically significant at the highest level. This would be a very high percentage of "super" hits in a normal reading; it is extraordinary for a "pre-reading."

He further stated,

> These analyses cannot (and should not) be dismissed as being based on ratings performed by naïve judges. These findings cannot (and should not) be dismissed as being based upon vague or general information (e.g. comparing the scoring for Wolf versus the cousin/control). Finally, this pre-reading cannot (and should not) be dismissed as the result of fraud. Such arguments are completely without merit in this instance. The scientific evidence is simply too overwhelming. When other evidence presented is taken into account, a compelling argument can be made that Wolf's efforts to communicate with us through Suzanne deserve to be taken seriously and received with gratitude, awe, and celebration.

The visit from Wolf was only the start of my journey with that powerful soul. In addition to the evidence he brought through, he led me to uncover the reason for his visit—a powerful lesson for all of us about our existence in two worlds at once, our connection with all that is, and our purpose while here in physical form. The evidence from Wolf's soul is what allows even skeptics to sit up and pay attention to these important messages. And yet, as accurate as his visit was, after Wolf visited me, I had yet another unexpected visit that proved to be even more accurate.

I received a call from Dr. Schwartz some time after Wolf's appearance asking me to do a reading for a gentleman as a favor for him. I agreed and set a time later in the week with Jerry Facciani. I knew nothing about Jerry or whom he had lost. Just as with Wolf's visit, I unexpectedly received a visit in the early morning hours from a woman whom I sensed was this Jerry's deceased wife.

The woman in spirit proceeded to give me a long list of evidence about herself, including her name. I typed my notes and sent them to Jerry, who was quite stunned by my unexpected communication prior to his reading. I asked him not to comment on any specific details, but to give me a one-sentence reply as to the information received. He replied that it was clearly a visit from his wife.

Because Dr. Schwartz had requested this reading, I asked Jerry to score the evidence and send the results to Dr. Schwartz to be tallied. As in Wolf's case, Jerry was asked to choose a woman still living to serve as a "control." He chose his current wife and scored each line item to determine how well the information matched her as compared to his deceased wife, whom I knew had visited me.

The results of scoring the items for his current wife were 35 percent clear misses. Thirty-six percent were meaningful, with a smattering of other "hits."

When we compare that with the scoring for the evidence I received in the unexpected visit from Jerry's deceased wife, with no feedback, we find that the results are dramatically different. There were no misses, none rated as a "stretch," none rated as a "possible hit," 5.9 percent rated as probably a hit, 8.8 percent rated as definite hits, and 85 percent rated as meaningful evidence.

Dr. Schwartz' commented, "A 'very conservative' percent accuracy score would be calculated using only the number of items scored 6, divided by the number of total items scored, and then multiplied by 100.

Using this formula, the very conservative percent accuracy rating for this pre-reading for M is 85.4%. Gary E. Schwartz has never before analyzed a reading receiving such a high percent accuracy score using the very conservative formula."

Then he rated all items considered probably hits or higher and had this to say about the results: "A less conservative percent accuracy score would be calculated by summing the number of items rated 4, 5 and 6, divided by the number of total items scored, and then multiplied by 100. Using this formula, a less conservative accuracy rating for this pre-reading for M turns out to be 100%. Gary E. Schwartz has never before analyzed a reading receiving a score of 100%."

He further stated, "It should be acknowledged that in the history of mediumship research, this apparent "double-deceased" spontaneous pre-reading is potentially historic and deserves to be so appreciated."

I joke that I was always an "A" student, and the spirit world knows that I wouldn't be satisfied with anything less, and so they give me this kind of evidence.

I went on to give Jerry his "live" reading by telephone two days later. Keep in mind that I deliberately kept myself blind to the accuracy of the pre-reading visit. During his reading, I sensed not just his wife, but one of his daughters and his beloved grandmother. I must tell you that Jerry's story was by far the most tragic I have encountered in a field that exposes its practitioners to a lot of grief. It turns out that Jerry's wife took her own life by asphyxiation. In the process, two of their children were asphyxiated along with her and the third almost died. Jerry came home to find this tragedy after the fact.

Here are the results of that phone reading. Because I communicated with three spirits during the reading, Jerry was asked to choose three women who are of a similar age to the ages of the deceased to serve as controls. He chose his current wife, his paternal grandmother, and his current wife's seven year old granddaughter. For the controls, most of the items would have been misses, had the reading been for any of these women.

And here is how the evidence was scored for the actual spirits who came through, along with Dr. Schwartz' comments:

> The findings for the scheduled phone reading generally replicate and extend the observations made for the spontaneous pre-reading. The overall reliability of SG's ability to receive accurate information (1) spontaneously (i.e. in the pre-reading) for a single spirit (M) in the absence of any possible cues or feedback from a sitter, and (2) during a scheduled time (i.e. in the phone reading) for three separate Spirits in the presence of a sophisticated and cautious sitter is clearly evident.

I want to stress that I do not get this kind of result every time. Because I keep detailed records of the evidence, I can tell you that 5 percent of my readings do not go well, for whatever reason, but happily the rest are at least 75 percent accurate, if not much higher. The reasons for that go beyond the scope of this paper. The point here is that when we ask for good evidence and have the commitment to accept nothing less, the spirit world provides.

Why is the evidence so important? For the healing it provides. For 33 years, Jerry Facciani carried around questions that were answered in the visit of his wife's spirit. This is a man who spent his entire career working with numbers and statistics, but in his case the reading did not just provide a preponderance of evidence, but what our judicial system calls evidence "beyond a reasonable doubt"—which is the highest standard used as the burden of proof. As a result, the reading was life-changing for him.

I have had quite a few clients come to me who are grieving over the loss of a beloved pet. It would be very easy to say, "Yes, your cat is here and she loved you very much." That is a nice message, but a medium and their client should not be satisfied with that. Pets have souls just like people do. The soul does not communicate in words; it communicates in concepts that the human brain translates into words. Knowing this, there is no reason why a medium can't ask the soul of a departed pet for evidence to leave their owner convinced that they are here and loved them very much.

The first time a woman asked me to connect her with her cat, I inwardly groaned. My initial thought was, "How am I going to get evidence from a cat?" I shrugged my shoulders and said, "OK, cat. You need to tell me all about yourself." And that's exactly what she did. I immediately sensed a female tabby cat that my client had had since she fit in the palm of her hand. The cat showed me the number 18, which was exactly how old she was when she died. When I asked the cat to show me the cause of death, I related to my client that the cat was sneezing and coughing. She confirmed that the cat had died of pneumonia.

As further evidence, the cat showed me that her owner had taken her everywhere she went, including for rides in the car. I don't know of any cat owners who do this, but my client did. This turned out to be a great piece of evidence for the woman for whom the cat had been like a child. She was weak with relief to learn that her cat was fine and that she would see her again.

I had a female client who was suffering from tremendous guilt over having to put her dog down. The dog showed me that he had been very docile around her, but quite aggressive and protective when anyone came near her. He then showed me that a man had broken into the woman's apartment and he frightened him off. I then sensed from this dog that the woman had been addicted to prescription drugs and was high when this incident occurred. He then showed me that the event so frightened the woman that she got clean from the drugs after the incident. She confirmed all of these details, and I told her that in effect, the dog's aggressive actions had saved her life. Because of this evidence, when I gave her the message that the dog didn't want her to feel guilty because she was now free of drugs, she knew the message came from her companion and not from me.

The stories I've shared with you are heart-warming and affirming, but what about when a life is in the balance? Can evidence help with that?

I was recently contacted by a woman whom I will call Peggy. She asked if I could listen to the soul of a friend of hers who had been in a coma for three weeks. She said the woman's eyes were moving under her lids, but the doctor told them she would likely not wake up. Her friends wanted to know what the woman's end of life wishes were. My initial reaction was not to want anything to do with this situation. I did not want what I sensed through a method of communication that is far from perfect to be used as the basis for a life-and-death decision.

Then I realized that if the woman in a coma could give me a preponderance of evidence with a high level of accuracy, I would be able to trust whatever messages she shared about her end of life wishes. I went into my study and set the intention of connecting with the soul of "the friend of Peggy's who is in a coma." I immediately sensed a presence, and asked her to tell me things that would convince me I was indeed communicating with her.

She proceeded to tell me her coma was the result of a clot, not trauma. She told me her mother's name, showed me people singing to her in the hospital and praying around her in a circle. She described her personality and education level in detail, and talked about a "red hair near her" and braids in her hair. She showed me a pair of funny striped socks that would be significant to someone close to her. She told me the name of the university with which the hospital where she was staying was affiliated. All of these facts were validated by Peggy.

Based on this evidence, I felt comfortable sharing the message that the woman already had one foot in both worlds and was enjoying playing on the other side. She was well aware of what was going on around her. She said it was OK to take her off the machines. If it was her time to go, she would go. If not, she would stay.

The funny socks turned out to be very significant. She had given them as a gift to the one person who was spending the most time with her in the hospital. He was also the person who was the most skeptical of mediumship.

There was one piece of evidence that was the most stunning of all. The woman's soul had said to me, "California here I come, right back where I started from." After Peggy shared all of the information with the circle of friends, one of them wrote to me. He said that he was still reeling over the California comment. It seems that he had been offered a job back in California where he had come from before moving to the state where he was now. None of his friends knew about the job offer, and he was unsure of what to do about it. He told me that the two items foremost in his prayers for the past three weeks had been the woman in the coma and the job offer. In fact, he half-playfully had asked the woman in the coma if she could get some higher guidance about his job offer and let him know. When he read my notes that she had said, "California here I come, right back where I started from," he was stunned.

Five days after this communication, the woman's spirit came to me unbidden during my morning meditation. She said to me, "It's beautiful here. I only wish everyone weren't so sad. They don't need to cry for me." I sent these messages to her friends, only to find out that the woman had passed to the other side six hours earlier. She came to let them know she was fine.

What does this mean for all of us? The soul is in both worlds at once at all times. It has access to far greater information than we do at the human level.

We are dealing with intelligence when we connect with the non-physical reality. Those of us who communicate with the other side need to constantly seek to raise the bar—to raise the level of credibility of that communication. If those of us who communicate with the other side do not take advantage of that fact and use it to bring greater awareness of this greater reality to others, then we are not honoring those who are doing their best to help all of us wake up to who we really are. It is the evidence that allows us to trust when dealing with things we cannot prove.

The keys to receiving more evidential communication are understanding that we are dealing with intelligence on the other side and that this is two-way communication. "Ask and you shall receive." We should not be satisfied with messages that leave room for doubt. We should ask for evidence in addition to messages. I have a list of the basic/bare minimum of evidence I would like those in the spirit world to give me in a reading and I make it my intention to receive everything on that list each time I do a reading. I then ask the spirits I'm working with to go beyond that list and knock my socks off with the evidence they can provide.

Our world is in great need of healing. Mediumship can offer that, but mediumship goes far beyond letting those left behind know that their loved ones are still very much with them. When practiced with the goal of achieving the highest level of accuracy and a preponderance of the evidence, mediumship can serve to show that

~   consciousness extends beyond the brain and exists
     independent of it

~   this aspect of consciousness is eternal in nature

~   all things are interconnected in the grand web of creation

~   the organizing principle of the cosmos and the overarching
      purpose of evolution is unconditional love

By my way of thinking, there is no greater service than to help
people awaken to these truths.

Bibliography:

Giesemann, Suzanne: www.LoveAtTheCenter.com
Giesemann, Suzanne (1998). *Conquer your Cravi*ngs. McGraw Hill
Giesemann, Suzanne (2007). *It's Your Boat Too.* Paradise Cay Publications
Giesemann, Suzanne (2008). *Living a Dream.* Paradise Cay Publications
Giesemann, Suzanne (2011). *Messages of Hope: The Metaphysical Memoir of a
      Most Unexpected Medium.* One Mind Books
      Giesemann, Suzanne (2009). *The Priest and the Medium.* Hay House
Giesemann, Suzanne (2012). *The Real Alzheimer's: A Guide for Caregivers
      That Tells It Like It Is.* One Mind Books
Giesemann, Suzanne (2011). *Through the Darkness.* (ghost written for Janet
      Nohavec) Aventine Press
Giesemann, Suzanne (2011). *Where Two Worlds Meet.* (ghost written for Janet
      Nohavec) Aventine Press
Giesemann, Suzanne (2013). *In the Silence: 365 Days of Inspiration from Spirit*
Tymn, M. (2014, April). Being Skeptical of Skeptics. *The Journal for Spiritual
      and Consciousness Studies,* 37(2), 61-64.

Biography

Suzanne Giesemann is the author of eleven books, a spiritual teacher,
and an evidential medium. She captivates audiences as she brings hope,
healing, and comfort through her work. Suzanne's gift of communication
with those on the other side provides stunning evidence of life after
death. Touted as "a breath of fresh air" with "a quality that is so different
from others that it is difficult to describe," she brings messages of hope
and love that go straight to the heart. Suzanne is a retired U.S. Navy
Commander. She served as a commanding officer, as special assistant to
the Chief of Naval Operations, and as Aide to the Chairman of the Joint
Chiefs of Staff on 9/11. Today Suzanne addresses questions about the
purpose of life, the nature of reality, and attuning to higher
consciousness. Her work has been recognized as highly credible by
afterlife researcher Dr. Gary Schwartz, Ph.D., and best-selling author Dr.

Wayne Dyer. She serves on the executive council of <u>Eternea</u>, where she is the chairman of the Spirituality Leadership Council.

Automatic Writing

Irma Slage

Abstract

This paper contains an excerpt from the book <u>Afterlife Communication: 16 Proven Methods, 85 True Accounts</u>. It begins with a description of how Irma Slage realized that she could do automatic writing. This form of communication, with her deceased mother, led to other forms of communication. Irma began to hear communication through her mind, see spirits clearly, and learn about the psychic world through those she met who passed on. The paper ends with instructions in how to use automatic writing to communicate with loved ones who have transitioned to the other side of life.

Communication Using Automatic Writing

by Irma Slage

From the book *Afterlife Communication: 16 Proven Methods, 85 True Accounts* (2014, pp. 146-161)

When my mother Sophie died of a sudden heart attack in her Philadelphia, Pennsylvania, home, my own life seemed to end as well. My mom. Always there for me. Always a supportive friend. Always so gentle and so strong. Always so firm, yet considerate and thoughtful and forgiving.

While sitting in my living room, alone in my darkness, I suddenly felt the need to pick up a pen, then paper. I started to write the capital letter "G." It was curved in a very round, artistic, distinctly creative way. We each have our own way of writing the letters. This was definitely not the way I would form the capital letter "G."

111

The following weekend, I went to my mother and father's house to help my dad. I was cleaning my dad's kitchen when my eyes were drawn to a corkboard my mother had hanging on the wall for phone messages. It was near the phone, not far from the kitchen sink where I was standing. For some unknown reason, I had put the paper with the capital letter "G" I had written in my pants pocket. I pulled it out and compared it to the writing on the corkboard. The "G" on the board and the "G" on the paper in my hand were written exactly the same.

Excitement filled my shaking body as I called to my husband, who was in the next room.

"Ted!"

He came running as if from the tone of my voice something was terribly wrong.

"What is it?"

"Look at this." I tried to control the excitement in my voice. "The 'G' I showed you last night and the 'G' written on this paper by my mother are exactly the same."

He took a closer look at the writing on the paper in my hand and then at the paper on the wall.

"They are the same," he said.

I said, "Look at the way the 'G' is sort of rounded at the top, then squares off.

He looked again.

"They are the same," Ted remarked.

While I was almost jumping with excitement, my husband appeared shaken, with a little less color in his face and a great deal of concern for our sanity.

"What do you think of that?" I asked.

"I don't know. It is the same, that's for sure," he said reluctantly.

"It must be my mother trying to tell me she can use my hand to form letters."

"It seems so," Ted answered.

My husband was a skeptic back then and didn't want to believe that my mom was contacting me. I believe it frightened him.

"When we get home, I'll try again," I said.

Later that night, I got a paper and pencil, sat down on a comfortable chair at my kitchen table with the paper in front of me and pencil in hand, and immediately the pen began to move. I watched in astonishment.

"Hi, Irma. I'm glad you understood the message from the capital letter 'G.'"

"That was you writing with my hand?"

"Yes," the pencil wrote.

There was no doubt that the person was my mother. I don't know how I knew; I just felt it.

"Are you all right?"

"Yes, everyone here is loved. It is so beautiful. Don't worry about your dad. He will be fine. It makes me sad to see him walking around that big house by himself."

Tears came to my eyes. I was very worried about my dad, dependent on my mother for so many years. They just celebrated their fortieth wedding anniversary.

"He'll be fine," my mom wrote again.

We communicated for another few minutes.

"Mom, is there something you can tell me that will prove that this is really you?"

The pencil wrote, "I took care of the dolls you had as a child. I bought them new shoes and socks. I washed their dresses. Take them home with you. Don't leave them in your dad's house."

"I will," I promised, speaking out loud.

I sat back in my chair. I felt so relaxed, as though I had taken a nap.

I stared at the writing on the paper. The handwriting was not mine. My handwriting is much smaller and bolder. The writing on the paper was shaky and irregular, and all of the words ran together. I had to make notes so I could remember some of my questions and fit them to the answers.

I didn't know it at the time, but writing through the pencil in this way is called automatic writing. Since then, I've read many books on it. Many people can do it and are not aware of their ability.

My father had Alzheimer's, and on his bad days on Earth when he appeared not to know what he was doing, his spirit body was sitting in my house enjoying my family and talking to me. On those days when he appeared to be coherent on Earth, he was mostly in his body.

My father's spirit continued to communicate through my automatic writing while he was still on the Earth plane with Alzheimer's. The one thing he wrote with my hand many times when he visited me in his spirit form was how unhappy he was to go back to his body on Earth and that he wanted to stay in the spirit world. He was so sad for years. Then one day he came to me and he was smiling. I could tell he was happy, but he didn't say why. Within a month he broke his hip and after a successful operation, died suddenly. He came to see me after he died, a very happy and relieved man, filled with the wonder of his new life.

In my book, written through automatic writing, a man wrote through my hand telling me much the same thing as my dad. He expressed it word by word. He wrote,

> My following feelings are mine alone. I was never in my body during the times it appeared. I had no memory or thoughts. I was not there. I was here watching people trying to control their tears and frustration. Then, when I finally left for the last time, when my time to stay in the world had come to an end, I knew it in advance and was very happy. I can't tell you how happy I was to be leaving that body for good.

He went on to say through the automatic writing,

> My life here continues in a helpful way to those who need me. For as I see a person going through what I did with Alzheimer's, I tell him to hold on because the end is near and the end is always here in a place where we can continue.

Our loved ones always hear us when we think of them, no matter how much time goes by. It brings to mind a young mother I helped on Earth. She lost her husband when he was flying in a small aircraft and it crashed.

"Oh well," she said, "It's been so many years he probably doesn't think of me anymore."

Her husband then spoke to me through automatic writing and I gave her messages from him that meant something to both of them. It was descriptions of things between them that I wouldn't know anything about. It showed her that our loved ones are never far from us.

Through automatic writing many of the people I write with who have died at an older age prefer to be about thirty years old in the spirit world, or any age that makes them feel comfortable. The first time I saw my elderly great aunt after death, she appeared to be in her late 20s and I didn't recognize her, but still, somehow I knew who she was.

Most of us know someone who has taken his or her own life. I didn't until 1977. Until then, people on Earth had told me that because these people took their own lives, they were in a terrible place so they would pay for doing such an awful thing. Here's what I've seen for myself.

His name was Lou, a neighbor who was five years younger than I was. He had marriage problems that he could not handle, and he hanged himself. I was sitting at my kitchen table crying after hearing this news, when I looked up toward my kitchen light fixture on the ceiling. Lou was looking down at me. He was a very bright light. He wanted me to stop crying because of him. With my pen on paper, he wrote that if I had died first and had come back and saw him crying, I would feel terrible; that's how he feels.

I stopped crying and stood up closer to where he was. My sadness stopped and in its place was one of the greatest joys I ever felt. I asked him if he was OK, because I heard that people dying as he did were in a terrible place.

He continued to write that he was in a beautiful place surrounded by love and not to worry about him.

There are times when spirits can use their energy to move physical things on Earth, including a pen to paper. I've heard these stories from people I have helped and they know the person who is moving the object. Generally, it is close to the person's funeral, or when a problem comes up that concerns them or someone they love, or even to let us know they are with us. They may push a picture to the floor, or make a light go on and off. In my case, I've had doors slam shut and open in my house. I felt my mom's arms around me as she hugged me after she died. And when I put her wedding ring on my right ring finger, I felt a jolt of electricity as she put the ring on my finger with me.

My husband, Ted, felt a special connection with a friend of ours after he left Earth. When I showed him my technique to have him use automatic writing, the person who wrote through my husband's hand was Owen.

It was years before this when I heard that my friend Owen was in the hospital. The first thing I did was talk to him through my mind. I can talk to anyone, living or deceased, including pets.

Shortly after his surgery, I asked Owen if I could help and what he would want most. He told me he wanted to go home. I then worked through my guide to get him well enough to go home. It was wonderful to know that he got his wish and was doing well. That was short lived, because soon after, he was taken back to the hospital with complications.

His health went up and down, and during this time I was in constant mental communication with him, making sure that he got plenty of help from the spirit world and that he knew I was trying to get him home once more.

In talking things over with some friends of ours, everyone knew that, in all probability, Owen would not make it through this illness. I felt Owen next to me at that moment and knew that he was counting on me to help get him out of the hospital once more. I asked all the people who have power on the other side, and one day as I sat typing, I heard a very nice voice in my mind say, "You don't know what is best for the people you are trying to help. Please know that you can't change anything this time."

The spirits were very nice but firm on this. I knew then that Owen was not going to make it, and I also knew that I was not to ask anything else of them.

A couple of days later, I was putting something on a low bench that is in my bedroom. As I bent over, I felt as though I had stopped in midair, body forward, and I had the feeling that time had ceased. As I stood up, I knew that a male spirit was behind me. I looked at the clock and it was 6:40 p.m. Later that evening, I received an email from his wife, Arlene, saying that Owen had died that night at 6:40. I felt elated that he had come to see me shortly after passing and that he knew I had tried to help and didn't feel that I had failed him. That would not have been Owen anyway. He was someone I was lucky to know.

Years later, I asked the other side for help as we struggled through a problem. The response came from Owen to Ted and me using automatic writing. He wrote that all will be well, and that he is with us.

While our life continues on Earth, as well as after we die, I felt that being one with each other is the most important concept of the books I wrote. We certainly felt one with Owen; he understood our problem and reached out to help.

Stories showing that we are all one in my first book, *Phases of Life After Death—Written in Automatic Writing,* are written by the spirits of men, women, and children of all ages, races, and religions. They came from different countries and backgrounds.

They may have been rich or poor. They may have been powerful people, or average people while on Earth. All of them have one thing in common: the memories and emotions of the life they just left.

In writing these stories using automatic writing, and as I transcribe these stories, I feel that all of the writers are trying to help us by giving us insight into their world as we continue our life on Earth. They want us to read their stories and keep them in mind as we experience our lives here.

Some of these people will give you memories that will stay with you for a long time, such as the young soldier who was in the Vietnam War. I will remember his story always, because I saw his face in front of me while he was using my hand to write. He was a tall black man in his early 20s with kind eyes. While in Vietnam, he was part of a combat team that was completely wiped out. His description of watching his family as they got the news of his disappearance brought tears to my eyes.

Here are excerpts of his words as he had me write them on paper:

> I was a military man, complete with a rifle and a lot of
> other arranged equipment. I am not certain of the passing
> of time but when I left my body, it did not seem as
> though a lot of time had transpired from the time I felt
> the pain in my shoulder. Other deceased soldiers were
> there with me, and one by one we were shown the way
> to a different spot. We drifted in different directions.
> One of the spots I was taken to was my mother's living
> room. There was a military man standing in the middle
> of the room dressed in his proper attire who came to give
> my mom my medal and tell her of my disappearance.
> The people who were in that room were the ones who
> mattered to me, and a few others, and they would find
> peace through each other.

Some of the people who spoke through my automatic writing in my book will be like people you know from personal experiences.

A man who had abused alcohol wrote through my hand that when he was on Earth he felt that his life was not worth anything. He found after his death that it wasn't true. The one person who needed him, his brother, learned most from him after he died. These are his words written through automatic writing:

> My brother was in the hospital trying to conquer alcohol.
> He was crying and grabbed my picture, holding it in his
> hands, and all in that room, including me, hovering
> beside his right shoulder, knew he wouldn't leave the
> facility again without winning his fight with alcohol. My
> picture never left his hands or his pocket in his pants. In
> death, I became his inspiration to get well.

And some of these people will take you through their own lives that may mirror your own. They are teachers. They will guide you as you read, just as they guided my hand and my heart as they wrote these stories.

They want you to remember them, and not to forget why we are on Earth and what our lives mean to each other.

We all have a continuation of life after the initial leaving of our bodies. Automatic writing gave me the opportunity to communicate with those people we can learn so much from.

That includes pets. Anyone who is close to their pet will tell you that communication between pet and owner is a very special bond. I give messages to people from their pets whether they are on Earth or have passed on. Messages about pets are also included in my book using automatic writing. This is one example of what was written as my hand was guided:

> My cat was taken away from me by death. No matter
> what happens to us, when a person or animal seems lost
> to us, that is not the way it is. The way it is is that we are
> connected to everyone. That's how we are still together.
> On the side I am on now, I just focus my mind on a
> person's name or an animal's name, and I have their
> locality.

Our life with people is interwoven. It is the same with our pets.

We are constantly communicating with the spirit world through our subconscious. Using automatic writing is one of those resources to bring those messages to our conscience mind.

An example of confirmation came when we first moved to the area where I live in California. A lot of information comes to me in the first five minutes of waking in the morning. We had just moved to a new city, and I felt I had to go to Castro Valley, California. I asked my husband how close Castro Valley was because I had never heard of it until that moment. I also got the names of streets to visit using automatic writing. I went on the Internet to find out how to drive to those streets. This is my interpretation of the reason this information came through and of what happened next.

Ted and I got in the car, and while Ted drove along the streets written on the paper I held, I did more automatic writing, asking the young spirit girl from whom I was getting the messages why we were going to where she was directing us. She wrote that I would find out soon. When we arrived at the street she had specified, we emerged from the car, not knowing what we were to see, and walked around. We noticed an in-ground water tank. Not seeing too much else, we got in the car and drove down another one of the streets she mentioned. I knew that street was significant to the young spirit with us, but I didn't know why, so I again wondered why we were there.

The next instruction from the deceased girl was to go to a nearby park. We parked and walked to a section of the park with small hills and valleys that had nothing on it. We stood there enjoying the view and thinking how nice it was. My husband and I enjoyed the beautiful summer day, but still did not understand why we were sent to these places in Castro Valley. I found out the next day when I went online.

I opened an email from Cheri, who told me about her young daughter, Valerie, who had recently died of cancer. The email was pretty long, and at the end she mentioned in that they used to live in Castro

Valley. I wrote Cheri back telling her the complete story of where we went and what we saw in Castro Valley and that we did not understand why we were there until her email. She wrote back and said that not many people who live in Castro Valley know about that water tank, which told her that we had walked around the area. The street we drove was the street where her family, including her deceased daughter, Valerie, lived while growing up. The park was shown to me because her daughter loved the hills and valleys that are there and the peacefulness that her daughter felt while looking at them.

Valerie's aunt wrote to me after buying my book. Using automatic writing, I wrote a letter to Valerie's aunt. The letter was signed, "Scarlett." I didn't know why until I received her aunt's email shortly after with the following explanation:

> I was filled with excitement to realize the identity of the Scarlett about whom you wrote. Valerie was fascinated with the movie, "Gone With the Wind," and had collected all the memorabilia, which Cheri has saved. What a validation. Who else would call herself Scarlett?" A Scarlett and Rhett Butler dancing figurine was given to Valerie by my mother-in-law many years ago, knowing her love for the movie. Cheri also reminded me of the Valerie-Scarlett connection.

Valerie, the young spirit girl who sent me to Castro Valley, found a way to let all of us know that she was with us. I used automatic writing to give her mother and her aunt messages from her, and those messages continue today. The spirit world is always helping us with many things.

Sometimes when people come to see me for a psychic reading, I give them a letter to take home with them using automatic writing. In a sitting with a woman, I gave her a letter to take to her sister who couldn't make the reading. I signed the letter, "Take it easy, Pal."

I didn't know why it was signed that way at the time, but I received an email later from the woman's sister telling me that her deceased father used to always say those same words when she left his house: "Take it easy, Pal."

You Can Use Automatic Writing

Automatic writing comes in many forms. It may come in drawings, numbers, or letters. You may be shown something in your mind like a picture; you may hear something in your mind like words; or you may feel an emotion. It may be none of these or all of these. Whatever it is, just write it down as you see it, hear it, or feel it.

While keeping our minds as clear as possible, our hand writes whatever comes across. I always start automatic writing by concentrating on writing a letter of the alphabet. From there, things take different paths for different people.

One example happened to a woman named Rhonda. When she put the pen to paper, she wrote the letter "M." The picture she formed in her mind was of her deceased mother, whose name was Marie. The picture was of her mother at a young age, in the house where she grew up. It gave her the emotions of love, comfort, and feeling calm. She reported feeling treasured, peaceful, and not alone. She had been thinking of her mother for the past week because Rhonda's husband had just passed and she wanted her mother's comfort.

Another message through automatic writing came from her deceased husband. The message was "Love, time, live, happiness, and enjoy."

Rhonda felt it was from her husband and felt the message meant he will always love her and wanted her to find happiness and enjoy life.

When Alice came to do automatic writing, she had been thinking of her Uncle Dee who had passed away recently. The message she got through automatic writing was, "The bump is on the stairs. It has to do with something big."

Alice explained that her great, great Aunt Florence lived in a Victorian house in Monterey. Alice and her husband visited the front of the house a few years ago with a copy of the original picture that they gave to the current tenant. There were grey cement steps that were steep going up to the front door. Alice's great Uncle Dee had been there many times, as well as Alice. The house had been in their family for generations.

Alice felt that the bump on the stairs had to do with the conflict in the family through many generations.

She also said that while writing the message, she felt relaxed and open, and although it was two generations back, she felt as though all took place in the present.

Alice spoke to her spirit guide through automatic writing. Her guide described himself as an older male. She saw blue rays shooting out of his hands toward her as a healing. He wrote the names of colors on the paper for her to feel. He described them as orange, blue, and yellow. He also wrote, "Have fun. Soon. Good-bye."

In asking her how she felt during her automatic writing session, Alice described herself as feeling, "sad, like crying, when he said good-bye."

Her feeling was that the colors were energy levels for her to live by and that she had a physical healing. The next day, Alice said that she had a physical condition that was greatly improved.

When Pam came to me, I brought her down to a very relaxed physical state. I told her to write a letter in the alphabet that meant something to her. The letter that came on the paper was "A." Pam said it stood for "alligator." For some reason that word came to her with thoughts about her female cousin named Willie who died years before. When they were kids, they spent a lot of time together, including overnights. They would play cards and have fun. While sharing a bed, if a pillow went off the bed, her cousin would tell Pam that she was not allowed to get it because alligators were there. To this day she can't get her pillow if it falls off of her bed in the middle of the night.

When Albert came to do automatic writing, the message that came through was, "This is from David S. your friend. I am glad you know who I am. I am doing well. I hope to see you on this side someday. I am sorry that we didn't contact each other before." The picture in Albert's mind was of David 45 years ago when they were in high school together. He was happy to see David's face. The letter from him meant a lot.

Frank didn't have anyone in mind to speak to when he came to do automatic writing. The pen began to write, "My name is Alan. I am here to help you with your kids. Stay true to yourself. Enjoy life. Don't worry." Alan had died years before. Frank was worried about his kids and knew Alan had kids also that he had problems with.

An example of speaking with someone through automatic writing came from Jessie. Jessie was sad when he came to see me and needed someone to help him know that it was OK to be happy. His Uncle Simon had just passed to the other side. Jessie's pen went to his paper and it began to write, "This is Simon. We are all going to have fun today. Be upbeat and happy about everything and have a happy day. Listen to music, sing your favorite song, and dance to make you happy and forget." His Uncle Simon knew that Jessie enjoyed music and it made him happy to get that message.

When we are children, psychic occurrences seem natural. We don't give things like this a second thought. We don't know how different and special it is. As we grow older, we realize how important communication from the spirit world is, and it is nice to know that our loved ones are not far from us. Automatic writing is one way to give us the opportunity that opens up a new world.

How to do Automatic Writing

1. Find a quiet spot without distractions.

2. Sit at a table or desk where you'll be comfortable, with paper and pen (or pencil).

3. Concentrate on your breathing. Feel your breathing going in and out. After breathing in and out three times, tell yourself that all parts of your body are relaxed. It will take a few moments to clear your mind and your body by telling yourself to relax each part of your body. Starting with your head, say each part of your body in your mind as it relaxes. Say in your mind, head, neck, arms, hands, front and back, legs and feet. Go back to concentrating on your breathing and while breathing out, for that one second, think of nothing. When your body is breathing out for that one second clear your mind.

4. Touch the pen or pencil to the paper.

5. You can look at the paper or keep your eyes closed.

6. Think of a question that you may want an answer. You may not get the answer to the question you ask, and it is a starting point.

7. You may be shown something in your mind like a picture, you may hear something in your mind like words, or you may feel an emotion. It may be none of these or all of these. Whatever it is, just write it down as you see it, or hear it, or feel it.

8. While keeping your mind as clear as possible, let your hand write whatever comes across. If you have trouble getting started, start with concentrating on writing down a letter of the alphabet that first comes to your mind.

9. When it is done, look over what your hand has produced.

Bibliography

Hogan, R. (Ed.) (2014). *Afterlife Communication: 16 Proven Methods, 85 True Accounts*. Normal, IL: Greater Reality Publications.

Biography

Irma Slage is a psychic medium who has shared her abilities for over 30 years through her automatic writing, private and public readings and lectures, clearing negative energy from real estate, hypnosis workshops, group events, and helping law enforcement. She uses automatic writing as a tool to teach communication from the spirit world. She gives messages and comfort to those on Earth. Irma can see deceased individuals and hear their voices as if they were in the physical world.

Irma is the author of *Phases of Life After Death— Written in Automatic Writing*, an inspirational account by spirits who answer the questions about life after death written in automatic writing through Irma. Irma also authored the book, *Psychic Encounters—A Guide to Having Your Own Spirit Contact*, which tells about ways of having psychic communication.

She has been featured on NBC television, and led viewers on a psychic tour of the Winchester Mystery House in San Jose, California. She has also appeared on many radio and television stations and major national and local newspapers.

Irma uses her gift to help paranormal researchers investigating ghost hauntings. She is also enlisted by people who need her help to clear their houses of unwanted spirits.

Pendulum Communication

Carol Morgan

Abstract

This article is a description of the process through which Carol Morgan learned to use a pendulum to communicate with her son Mikey, living in spirit. Soon after Carol's son Mikey passed away, she and her family began to receive communications from him. She was eventually led to go to a workshop held by Sally Baldwin, of the Dying to Live Again Foundation. There, she learned how to use a pendulum to connect with Mikey. The messages were consistently brought forward with integrity and love. Over time, Carol began to realize she was hearing Mikey telepathically as the pendulum moved. Her telepathic ability continues to improve with practice, but the pendulum always gives Carol the validation she needed with the messages received. For this reason, the pendulum is a critical communication tool for Carol. Mikey's communication started out quite simple. He would tell her how much he loved her and his family. Mikey said that life is eternal and the "Heavenly dimensions" are all around us. Gradually, Mikey progressed with the knowledge he was giving Carol. He told her that they had a plan before they came to Earth to teach through the veil about the afterlife. That it is all about LOVE and love is very powerful! Mikey said he needed to leave when he did to fulfill this plan. Carol ends the article by listing the keys to success with using the pendulum to communicate with loved ones who have transitioned off of the Earth plane.

Carol Morgan is a happily married mother of two sons, one of whom passed into Spirit in 2007 at the age of 20. Her oldest son, Mikey, was killed in a jeep roll-over accident in the Colorado mountains at the beginning of his junior year of college. Awakened by the doorbell in the early hours the following morning by a policeman, paramedic, and minister, sent chills down Carol's spine. Their worst nightmare had happened. Carol and her husband Mike had physically lost one of their precious sons. Joey's brother and hero was no longer with him. The devastation and deep heartache that followed was unbearable. How could they ever survive without him? A huge part of their family was gone.

The heartache and fear extended to Mikey's friends who were present at the accident. However, there was never any blame or anger toward anyone. The Morgan family felt deep love and concern for them. They did all they could to help these friends get through this tragedy as well. Everyone was hurting and everyone made much effort to comfort one another.

Two years after Mikey's passing, Carol was one of seven mothers in the United States chosen by the Dying To Live Again Foundation to participate in a Mother-Child Reunion Retreat in Sun Valley, Idaho. The retreat was to focus on communication with their children who had passed into the afterlife. This foundation was started by Sally Baldwin who was a spiritual medium. It was at this retreat that Sally told Carol she had the ability to communicate with her son. Sally taught Carol how to communicate with Mikey by means of a pendulum. Without mediumistic abilities or any prior knowledge or skill, Carol has practiced her pendulum communication techniques so rigorously over the past four years that Carol and Mikey are now in regular contact. They work together to answer questions on Afterlifeforums.com and elsewhere, and provide detailed afterlife education for people from all over the world.

The Background of Carol and Mikey

Carol and Mike Morgan lived a regular life in Minnesota raising their two sons, Mikey and Joey. Carol worked part-time as a physical therapist at the local hospital, and tried hard to attend all the different activities her boys were involved in. They belonged to the Catholic Church and raised their sons with this belief system.

For years prior to Mikey's passing, the Morgan family would go to Colorado for skiing and snowboarding vacations. As they drove up Interstate 70 to Copper Mountain, it was tradition to play the John Denver CD and sing "Rocky Mountain High" at the top of their lungs! Mikey always said that his friends would probably make fun of him if they knew how much he liked John Denver music. It was Mikey's love for snowboarding and the mountains that brought him out to Colorado for college.

Mikey loved life and was very involved in activities. Mikey had a smile that would light up any room. His beautiful auburn hair curled out from underneath the MN Twins baseball cap he always wore. Mikey was in the business school at CSU and was focusing on marketing. He loved to listen to music and had great interest in the messages that songs would give. He pursued this interest and ended up working as a DJ at the popular restaurant and bar near campus. Mikey worked hard at this job, eventually getting to be the main DJ on the big college nights. Though his song selection had to focus on the most popular tunes of the time, he had a few favorites that he played at every event he could. Bob Sinclair had written two songs that Mikey felt had some great lyrics with a strong message. "Love Generation" and "World Hold On" talked about the importance of love, peace, and unity. "Love Generation" was Mikey's favorite song at the time of his passing. This song became his "trademark," and he pushed it out there for everyone to hear as much as he could. "Be the love generation, peace and love to everyone you meet.......look to the rainbows and you will see, the sun will shine to eternity!" Little did Carol know that Mikey was laying down the foundation of a bigger plan and message that was about to unfold.

Signs: The Beginning of Communication

Mikey passed into Spirit on September 22, 2007.

Almost immediately following the accident, Mikey began to give signs of his survival to Carol, his dad, and younger brother. As people found out what happened, they came over to the Morgan's house to help give comfort. One of the neighbors turned on the radio and John Denver was playing. Mike was outside crying for Mikey when he looked up to see the flag on the flag pole flapping in the wind, but there was no wind! Joey called Mikey's phone number with his cell phone and within a minute their house phone rang. When they picked up the phone, no one was on the line. This occurred at almost 11:00 pm. Joey knew Mikey had called him back! Friends and other family members were noticing signs and having dreams with messages as well. Hearts showed up on bowls coming out of the dishwasher and in the bottom of coffee cups. The kitchen light would go on and off by itself when someone would talk about Mikey. Vacuum cleaners of friends and family were burning out the first week after Mikey's passing. He hated the sound of a vacuum! And he was making it clear he still did!

The most significant sign for Carol occurred three days after the accident, again two days later, and then again when she was in stores as time went on. After Carol found out about the accident that caused Mikey's passing, when one of Mikey's friends called from Colorado, she asked him if he would please send home Mikey's treasured baseball cap. She felt if she could not have Mikey, at least she could have and hold his beloved cap. His friend said he had the cap and would send it to Minnesota with some of his clothes. After planning the funeral and arriving home to a kitchen full of people, Carol noticed a box on the counter that was delivered to the house while they were gone. She opened the box to find the MN Twins Baseball cap sitting on top of some of Mikey's clothes. Carol grabbed the hat holding it and smelling it. She took the hat over into the bay window area with Mike and Joey following her. The sky suddenly opened up on this heavy overcast day, with sun rays beaming in strongly into the kitchen. The warmth was tremendous with a strong feeling of Mikey's presence. Carol hollered to everyone, "I can feel him! I can feel Mikey! He's here! I know it!" As she said this, a song was playing in the background by John Denver. When the song finished, the sun went under the clouds and the feeling of Mikey's presence was gone. Carol began to weep with heartache. A strong feeling of concern filled the room. One of Carol's friends said to her, "Did you hear that song? It was "My Sweet Lady" by John Denver. Mikey was using that song to talk to you." Carol could not remember the lyrics, so she got out the CD and replayed the song. The words described how she felt perfectly, and Mikey was making it clear that he was as close as he could be.

Two days later, Carol was sitting at the kitchen table with Mike and Joey getting pictures ready for the video Mikey's friends were putting together for the funeral. They were listening to music on the CD player trying to calm themselves. The player was full of discs with the music on full shuffle. The doorbell rang and Mike got up to answer the door. When he got there, all that was at the door was a box with no return address. As Mike stood holding the box at the door, Carol suddenly noticed the song that was starting to play. It was "My Sweet Lady" by John Denver. Carol told Mike to hurry and open the box. She became frantic about it as the song played. When Mike opened the box, inside it was Mikey's original Minnesota Twins baseball cap. It was all worn out and Carol thought Mikey had thrown it away because he had received a new one for his birthday that year . Carol knew that hearing the song "My Sweet Lady" each time Mikey's treasured caps arrived was Mikey trying to communicate with her!

This song played over the PA system when Carol walked into Walgreens; it played when she went to Joann's Store to buy decorations for Mikey's gravesite. The song followed her for two years until she met Sally Baldwin. The lyrics of this song were so powerful, it was as though the song had been written for Carol. The words described her tears and heartache as she grieved for Mikey, but she needed to understand that their lives were now joined and entwined. Truly, their time was just beginning.

Carol was having dreams of Mikey that were so real she could feel him. He would talk to her and tell her he was not really gone. "I can hear you, Mom, when you talk to me!" Carol also felt she could hear Mikey's voice at times during the day. But she put that off to wishful thinking and that it was probably her imagination.

Events that Led Carol to Meet Spiritual Medium Sally Baldwin

During the first year after Mikey's passing, Carol attended meetings with Compassionate Friends, a grief support group for parents who have lost a child. During one session, she met Mitch Carmody. He was presenting on Whispers of Love which was about signs from our loved ones who had passed into the afterlife. Carol was thrilled about this presentation as it confirmed to her what was happening was real. It was not a coincidence like some folks told her. Mitch asked if anyone in the audience had a sign to share. Carol got up in front and talked about two different signs she received from Mikey. After the presentation, Mitch asked Carol if he could publish one of her stories in his column in the *Living With Loss Magazine*. Carol agreed and one of her stories was published. A few months later when the magazines arrived, Mitch called Carol to tell her she could pick up some extra copies at his house. When Carol arrived at Mitch's house to get the magazines, he looked at her and said, "I just received an e-mail from Sally Baldwin from The Dying To Live Again foundation. She is recruiting moms from all over the United States for an all-expense paid trip to Sun Valley Idaho for a Mother-Child Reunion Retreat. She is picking up to ten mothers. It is based on communication with signs and dreams. Carol, I am tingling all over! You need to apply for this! You have had so much going on with signs and dreams." Mitch gave Carol Sally's email address. When Carol got home, she contacted Sally and told her about all her experiences.

A few days later, Sally contacted Carol and asked her to fill out the application for the retreat. Many mothers applied. Within a couple weeks, Carol was told she was accepted. The retreat was to be held in October of 2009. Being raised Catholic, Carol suddenly felt hesitant. She was excited but also scared that she had been picked. She decided to go see her elderly cousin who was a practicing Catholic nun to ask her what she thought. She had been so loving and helpful with Carol since Mikey's passing. This cousin was a strong believer in signs and dreams as communication. She also believed some mediums truly had the gift to communicate directly with our loved ones. This nun told Carol she needed to attend the retreat. She felt what was happening to Carol was real and she was picked for a reason. This gave Carol the confidence she needed. Carol attended the retreat bringing her husband for comfort. He did not attend the event, but did other activities during the day, and had profound signs of his own during this time.

The Retreat with Spiritual Medium Sally Baldwin

The retreat was held at a beautiful resort in the mountains of Sun Valley. Carol met the staff of the retreat that included Sally Baldwin, her husband Steve, grief counselors, Reiki and healing touch practitioners, massage therapist, and other loving supporters. All the mothers met on the first day together as well. Sally discussed the format for the retreat. She first focused on signs and dreams as communication.

The second day, Sally did private readings for each of the mothers. It was during this session that Sally told Carol she had the ability to communicate with her son Mikey. Sally said that Mikey was of a high energy and had great ability. Sally told Carol that Mikey was persistent in getting his mother to this retreat and that he had communicated with her. She said the fact that Carol never held blame or anger to anyone involved in the accident, including God, was just not the norm. She told Carol because of your loving connection with your son and the fact she held no blame or anger, she had the ability to communicate with Mikey, and she would show her how by means of a pendulum.

Pendulum Communication

The days that followed, Sally taught the seven mothers who attended the retreat how to use a pendulum for communication. She gave each a pendulum and a colored disk that had the alphabet and numbers 0 through 9 on the outer edge of it. The mothers sat at a large table, each working with their pendulum and disk. Sally had the mothers ask for God's loving guidance as they learned to communicate with their children.

The mothers needed to determine how the pendulum would move for the answer "yes" and then the answer "no" by their child. Carol asked Mikey how he would move the pendulum for her. Mikey moved the pendulum clockwise when Carol said the word "yes', and counter-clockwise for the word "no." This was a miracle for Carol! She could literally see the energy move and change the movement of the pendulum with each question. After this was confirmed, Sally told the mothers to center the pendulum on the disk, and to ask their child to spell a message. For Carol, the pendulum started to swing up toward the letter L. When she lifted the pendulum over this letter, Mikey moved the pendulum in a clockwise motion confirming "yes" to this first letter. Carol then centered the pendulum again on the disk and it started to swing up to the letter O. When Carol moved the pendulum over this letter, again Mikey circled it clockwise confirming "yes" to the second letter. This pattern continued until Mikey spelt the word love. When Carol asked him if this word was correct, he swung the pendulum greatly in a clockwise motion confirming "yes." Tears began to roll down Carol's cheeks. She could hardly believe it; she was actually communicating with her son! She could "see" what he was saying! Sally had the mothers practice by asking their children simple questions and working on getting the answers with the pendulum and disk. It was truly an emotional experience.

When Carol returned home, she was excited and fearful. Who would believe this? Her husband supported her, and he too was amazed by the whole thing. She was cautious on who she would share this with in the beginning. Carol practiced every day. She would call for Mikey and then ask for God's loving protection. She would ask Mikey questions and he would answer them by spelling out each word on the disk. It was obvious to Carol that it was her son as he "talked" just like he did when he was on Earth. One day as Carol practiced, the pendulum started to swing wildly at an angle, a direction it never moved before. When Carol asked Mikey what that meant, he said that is how he will move the pendulum when he is laughing. Soon the pendulum became much more animated with Mikey's humor!

As long as Carol continued to develop her pendulum communication in this way, messages were consistently brought forward with integrity and love.

As Carol improved with her skill, she began to experiment. She substituted coupons or a newspaper for the letter disk and had Mikey spell things with the pendulum. He did it successfully. She would put a key on a string and have Mikey move it in different directions. He could even move a full set of keys! Carol began to notice how precise the movement was becoming. Mikey was moving anything on a string. It did not matter what she used.

Over time, Carol began to realize she was hearing Mikey telepathically as the pendulum moved. As she continued to practice, Mikey would give her the first letter of the word, Carol would then say the word she heard, and Mikey would confirm by a "yes or no" movement of the pendulum as to whether she was correct. This made their communication much faster. If Carol made a mistake, Mikey would correct her and give her the letters until she had the right word. This continued to improve over time to the point where Carol could hear up to a sentence of information from Mikey. She would then say the sentence and Mikey would confirm if it was correct. He would also make any changes by spelling the corrections with the pendulum on the disk.

Her telepathic ability continues to improve with practice, but the pendulum always gives Carol the validation she needed with the messages received. For this reason, the pendulum is a critical communication tool for Carol.

Mikey's Messages

Mikey's communication started out quite simple for Carol. He would tell her how much he loved her and his family. Mikey said that life is eternal and the "Heavenly dimensions" are all around us. Mikey told Carol she would see him again and that their hug in the afterlife would be 100 times better than a hug on Earth! Death on Earth is only a temporary "physical" separation and we are still very connected with our loved ones. They do come to our important Earthly events and watch over us. They can see and hear us, especially as they draw close to this dimension. Mikey talked about the signs and dreams he gave her, confirming it was real communication. He talked about their dogs in the afterlife and how Chelsea, the golden retriever, still loved to play fetch with her ball. Mikey described the beautiful colors, scenery, and music he experienced. He said he was still snowboarding and was really good! Mikey told Carol he was wearing his baseball cap and that he looks exactly the same as the last time she saw him. He will feel and look solid. He just does not have his Earthly internal organs. Mikey told Carol we generally take on an "appearance" with our energy of when we looked good while we were here on Earth.

Gradually Mikey progressed with the knowledge he was giving Carol. He told her that they had a plan before they came to Earth to teach through the veil about the afterlife. That it is all about LOVE and love is very powerful! Mikey said he needed to leave when he did to fulfill this plan.

Mikey describes GOD as the Unity of Absolute Pure Love which is Infinite. It is the Collective, the Loving Force, the "Love Team" which we are all part of. He said God is beyond anything the human mind can comprehend. Mikey told Carol that God is not a man who sits in a big chair and judges people. God does not strike down on us. There is no eternal damnation. There is always loving guidance there to help souls progress themselves if they choose. God = LOVE. The more loving we are, the more "God-like" we are. It is truly a Unity of loving souls! Mikey said it is really all about love, kindness, forgiveness, and not judging others. We come to Earth for the experiences it offers to progress ourselves spiritually, and we may come several times.

Understanding Channeling /Soul Communication with Use of a Pendulum:

Keys to success:

1. Having a sincere loving intent to connect with a loved one

2. Truly believing that communication is possible

3. Allowing this to happen without fear

4. Letting go of anger and blame and other negative emotions that lower our vibration

We must clear our filters and blocks. It requires training, practice and dedication. It challenges us to think differently. It requires willingness. Channeling is all about sharing love and wisdom from those who are not separate from us!

Channeling/soul communication is not mysterious, spooky, or weird. Channeling is opening to a greater awareness of whom you are, your "other" half. Channeling is the love of God, the connection to our higher-self, the sacred benevolent connection to home, and a portal to our loved ones. It is realizing we are all part of the "Soup" we call God and we cannot ever be separated, even by death. We are so much grander and magnificent than our single-minded 3D perception has traditionally believed or allowed. We are divinity disguised as a human being.

Channeling is normal. From the beginning of humanity, it has been the way we have communicated, with our source of creation, things that needed to be delivered personally to us. It is guidance on demand. It is a beautiful system for us to communicate to them and them to us.

Channeling or soul communication can be experienced in different ways for different people whether it is by pendulum, signs, dreams, intuition, or meditation.

The pendulum is one tool you can use as you reconnect with your power, becoming aware of your greater self and your connection with your loved ones on the other side of the veil. The fact that everything is energy becomes apparent as you see the pendulum come alive with movement! The loving energy that flows proves that we are eternal beings forever connected with those we love in the dimensions all around us.

**Always understand that there are many ways we can connect
and communicate with our loved ones in the afterlife.**

Biography

Carol has been a physical therapist for over 29 years working with
patients with neurological disabilities. Her physical therapy work has
given her exposure to grief in all forms as well as grief from the passing
of a loved one. With this understanding, Carol has answered detailed
questions about the afterlife asked by people from all over the world
through radio interviews. Carol is a strong proponent of the knowledge
that signs from our loved ones in the afterlife are the lifelines that pull us
out of the pit of grief.

Carol has answered detailed questions about the afterlife asked by
people from all over the world through radio interviews and on
Afterlifeforums.com

The Making of a Medium: A Therapist's Perception

Karen Herrick, Ph.D.

Abstract:

From a psychological perspective, this paper tracks psychic ability from Franz Mesmer's (1724-1815) belief of Animal Magnetism, regarding the subtle fluid that permeates the universe, the planets and the central nervous systems of humans to promote through the "laying of hands" cures for physical ailments. The magnetic passes of his hands could induce trance-like conditions. After Mesmer helped us to understand altered states of consciousness, James Braid (1795-1860) brought us hypnosis which influenced Sigmund Freud (1856-1939) for a period of time. Carl Jung (1875-1961) studied Paracelsus (1493-1541), a distinguished Swiss physician, who believed that we attracted astral fluids which nourished our soul and that we could heal others through the use of these fluids.

Spiritualism, a Protestant-based religion that believed in communication with spirits, developed in the nineteenth century. Spiritism broke off from Spiritualism to add the concept of reincarnation and the concept of the perispirit, the fluid body of the soul responsible for transmission of thought from the ethereal to the material world. Thought communication bridges time and space interdependently between the physical universe where we live, the unobstructed universe where our soul goes between and after our lives, and the universe of God or the universal intelligence. The biggest difference is the frequency at which energy functions in these three areas.

These concepts weave through a story of a dysfunctional client who came into therapy because she was a single mom, came from an alcoholic home, was having parenting and work-related problems and was also seeing negative and positive spirits under her bed in the middle of the night.

The Making of a Medium:
A Therapist's Perspective

by Karen Herrick

A woman named Judy called the office one day and said she found my name on a psychic forum website. She was a single mom, came from an alcoholic home, was having parenting problems, and was seeing spirits under her bed in the middle of the night. Some of these spirits were not friendly. She said she knew I would understand because her positive spirits had told her that if I became her therapist I was going to be instrumental in developing this aspect of her life. Because of my Ph.D. work in *Naming Spiritual Experiences*, post-Ph.D. education that I continue to complete, and her humble attitude and honesty, I believed her.

Almost forty years ago, I had joined the Association for Research and Enlightenment (ARE), which is the foundation started to publicize the work of Edgar Cayce (1877-1945), the well-known American psychic. Every other month since then, I have received their magazine educating me on many different types of paranormal experiences.

Clients have told me many different stories about spirituality and/or paranormal events they have experienced. Then in 1987, I had my own spiritual experience where the Holy Spirit went through my body during a Holotropic Breathwork Experience (Grof, 1989). I eventually decided to apply for and complete a Ph.D. in *Naming Spiritual Experiences* where I studied the work of William James, Carl Jung, Abraham Maslow, and Stanislaw Grof. I completed research on approximately 130 mental health professionals who had many different types of positive personal spiritual experiences themselves and knew of many experienced by their clients.

Client Arrives for an Assessment Interview

Judy arrived a week later for her assessment appointment. My office is in the two-block "historic" section of the traditional-looking suburban town of Red Bank, New Jersey. She happily noted that there would be a lot of spirits in this historic section of the town. The session began with my taking a three-generational history of her and her family of origin. I then asked her to tell me what was going on in her life.

"I need to see you about everyday issues and there's a component of the supernatural. This 'stuff' just comes in. I've been getting some amazing premonitions which are really cool. Spirits sometimes float around me. That's cool too. I can't let my family know. Everybody in my family considers me weird. I'm the outcast of the family."

In Chapter 2 of my book Y*ou're Not Finished Yet*, the roles people take on in their family-of-origin are discussed. Judy was the scapegoat—the one who acts out in childhood and adolescence and shows hostility, defiance and anger for what's going on in the family. They usually have low self-esteem due to the anger and rejection they have received from relatives and their parents. She agreed that this was her role. Most of the therapy I did with Judy regarding her alcoholic and dysfunctional home can be better understood by reading *You're Not Finished Yet* (Herrick, 2007) in its totality.

Feeling different from other people is another trait that comes from living in an alcoholic and dysfunctional home. Since she had exhibited this from her dysfunctional childhood, it was probably easier for her in some way to try to understand and take in why she had been chosen for this "gift" of psychic ability because for most of her life she had felt she was different.

Negative Spirits Came In at First

"Yes, that was me. I was the scapegoat for sure and maybe some of the mascot which is the name for the family clown. If my family ever finds out I'm seeing spirits they'll try to take my twelve-year old son away from me. And, some of the spirits are creepy. Their energy feels different. I start to get frightening images in my mind. They have horror on their faces."

"I feel their resistance. Sometimes they nip at me. They make ugly faces. They are scary. With the good ones, I feel their ideas and they give me positive symbols." Judy also stated that she was reading inspirational literature daily in order to raise her vibration to be able to contact with higher spirits.

Judy stated that to rid herself of the negative spirits, she had a coach who was a medium herself, and the coach had suggested that she paint her bedroom blue. "My coach came to my house and was talking to her spirit guides and they told her to paint the bedroom a pale blue. I looked it up and the color blue emanates a calm and peaceful environment. It helps you go to sleep. In other diverse cultures, it brings peace and it is believed to keep the bad spirits away. Since I painted my bedroom, part of the craziness with the negative spirits has calmed down."

"My coach also told me of a positive mantra to say. It goes like this: 'Surround me with white light. I will not let anything through that does not belong to me. I cast out any feelings that are not my own and I do not invite any negative thoughts into my light." I also have been told to sprinkle salt on the arms of furniture at night and wipe or vacuum it off in the morning. The floor can be mopped with salt water or Holy Water which is just salt water that has been blessed. Salt breaks up the energy in the air in the room."

"Also regarding the negative spirits, I was making them stronger by being afraid. Even though we know they exist, it's just negative images in my mind. I am learning not to pay attention to everything that comes to me. Or, if I see a negative image, I can imagine that I have swords in both hands and I'm cutting up the negative images. (Author's Note: Jungian psychology believes that active imagination is one of the keys to use in creating a successful life.) That worked for me. The negative images/spirits went away."

"I was doing readings with people but those readings were just bringing the negative spirits in so I stopped. My medium coach said that I have to wait a year to actively seek readings again." I validated that it was excellent that she had stopped doing readings for people since one of the biggest lessons to learn when you have psychic ability is how to maintain boundaries around it and about it.

Psychic Ability Usually Is Inherited

I told Judy that many times psychic ability runs in families. Sometimes people don't understand what's happening and some of the family members think these people are "crazy" because they are not as rational as some of the other family members. The Swiss psychologist, Carl Jung, believed that we inherit traits from our ancestors. He also stated that we inherit jobs from them to finish in our life because they remained unfinished in their lives. Judy mentioned that she believed her grandmother had the gift of seeing spirits but she had never developed it and was pleased to learn that if she decides to become a medium, she could be finishing a family "job."

Spiritualism

Because of all this previous experience and because I had educated myself on the concept of the soul regarding Jungian and Transpersonal psychologies, I believe that a spirit is just a person, a soul and/or a Self without a body. Most religions believe in a soul but they do not educate people about it. I had also learned that Spiritualism was a religion, originated from Protestantism, which had added to this religion the belief in communication with spirits. Spiritualism also believes that even after death, the spirit can learn and grow on different levels and spheres in the afterlife. Spiritualism followers believe in reading literature in addition to the Bible and receive much of their information from spirits. In light of my background, I believed Judy when she said she was seeing dead people under her bed at night.

In Spiritualism, God is referred to as infinite intelligence and everything we experience in and about nature is taken as proof of this intelligence. Coming from an alcoholic home with a Catholic mother and a Protestant father, I hadn't believed in God. Neither of my parents went to church and I *knew* that God wasn't interested in what was going on in my home where there was constant fighting and chaos.

But in being raised in beautiful upstate New York, even as a child, I thought that there had to be something that was responsible for nature. I would walk in the woods for hours as a young adolescent looking closely at flowers, bushes and trees. This natural world made a great deal of sense to me in its beauty and calmness. I felt a presence there.

Some therapists due to ignorance about spiritual and paranormal events may have diagnosed Judy with mental illness even before meeting her. Maybe they would even have not taken her case.

Spiritism

Spiritism is a branch of Spiritualism that was developed by Allan Kardec (1804-1869), a French teacher and educator. The basic difference between Spiritualism and Spiritism is that Spiritism believes in reincarnation, which their followers state is needed so our knowledge can increase with the experiences from other lives (Limoges, 2014). Since I have experienced past-life memories, I identify with this belief in reincarnation increasing the knowledge of our soul.

According to Jon Aizpurua in his book entitled *Fundamentals of Spiritism, The Soul, The Afterlife, Psychic Abilities, Mediumship and Reincarnation and How These Influence Our Lives* (2013), "There are imperfect spirits who are those who have not yet left the realm around Earth. They still have their own issues or material interests which predominate over spiritual ones. Good spirits are those that practice good efforts and good works for the people they are helping. Pure spirits have reached the last level of intellectual and moral superiority. In asking for help, it would be good to call on pure spirits whenever possible. Spirits intuitively remember where they have lived, what they have learned in those lives that they lived in different cultures and they bring these remembrances to us by means of thought" (p. 195). The spirits Judy first experienced seem to be the imperfect ones.

Client Was Unhappy at Work

Judy also stated that she uses her psychic gifts on her job. "This woman has been hired as my superior. She was unhappy in another position with the company and asked to return to headquarters. She's bright, but abrasive and angry. She's been passed over for promotions she's wanted. My reputation in the company has been a positive one. I'm good at what I do. I treat others fairly. I keep to myself with little drama. This woman loves drama!

She's supposed to share my supervision with Joe, my previous supervisor who is a good friend. However, now all of my work goes through her. She told me to no longer copy him on any emails but to copy her instead. Any good ideas that have come from me she takes credit for as if they are hers. She says I make her feel uncomfortable and I need to treat her as if she's in charge because she is."

"The good spirits show me things like who's coming down the hall for a surprise visit so that I'm more prepared for what others will say to me or request. They give me images of people at work showing me the different emotion on their faces. Then I'm prepared for what kind of mood they will probably be in before I see them that day. Also, when I get a 'feeling' to check something related to work, I do it right away. When it comes to work, the words that keep coming into my head from the spirits are 'Protect Yourself.'"

How Did Psychic Ability Begin?

I asked Judy to tell me how she discovered she had psychic ability. I wanted to know why this was happening to her now. She stated, "About six months ago I was getting harassed at work, my son was failing at school and I just wanted to give up. I started to pray and ask, 'How come everything is hard for me? God you need to help me. Please, I need your help.' I said it night after night. I also, about the same time, stopped being addicted to food. I now believe my food addiction might have been blocking my intuitive sensing. Three months later, the spirits started appearing.

"I became physically ill the first few times I channeled the spirits. I start to feel electricity go through me when I begin to channel and the intensity of energy was really high in my body. Sometimes it felt like my arms and legs were going to be blown off. I absorb the energy of the spirits and also the energy of the person coming or calling for the reading so when I didn't throw up in the beginning I was just exhausted. The spirits first gave me words in big block letters and then soon after they started giving me images instead."

"When I get authentic information, it feels warm and solid. Sometimes the information feels phony and plastic and then I just don't take it in. When there's a spirit around who wants me to take in the information, I feel as if someone is physically there and I feel pressure around me."

"I went to a wake recently to support my friend and I didn't sleep well that night. There was this new spirit from the wake who was bothering me during the night. He didn't know 'my rule.' It is that spirits can't bother me between 11:00 at night and 6:00 in the morning. They have to talk to me during the day because I have a day job and I need my rest."

Receiving Communications

It is important that a medium receive evidence-based information that gives the person coming to receive the evidence that this information is from their loved one. Judy told me many stories where the people who she read for validated that this was their loved one. There were the usual examples such as these:

- "There is this red dress in the closet. In the pockets of the dress, you will find money. Your father hid the money in the dress and wants you now to find it."

- "Your mother hid money in the attic. It's in the part of the attic floor that's over the bathroom that has the claw-foot tub. 'Don't sell the house' she says 'until you find that money.'"

- "There's a black chest somewhere in the house. It's been moved around many times. Find it because there are important papers in there."

- "A spirit tapped me on the arm one evening and asked me to take down information for my friend who was his sister. He gave me his name and I wrote down the messages he wanted me to give her and they all made sense. She was so relieved he had thought to give her these messages as he had been estranged from the family when he died and the messages helped to explain a lot to her."

- "A friend asked me to look into her house and see what types of spirits were there. One of the spirits was a nun who had Jessica Lange's face. I didn't understand that until I learned that Jessica Lange is in a TV series and she's one of the most sinister characters in the show. My friend had sage burned in her house and it seems to have helped remove whatever sinister spirit/s were in there."

Mary Queen of Scots or Anne Boleyn

Almost all of what Judy had told me during the first few months had rung true for me. There was one story, however, that didn't seem to be so clear. It went something like this: "A woman named Mary showed up at my house one day. She was dressed in black, all ruffles down to her waist, with a long flowing skirt on her dress. She told me her name but she had no face. She said that I was safe and that I am loved and she didn't want me to let what's going on at work ruin my day. "We're taking care of you," she said. Then she showed me she had no head. When I asked her to tell me about herself I saw this amazing mansion that was blocks long. It was a castle. She had been absolutely ridiculously wealthy, whoever she was. The clothes she was wearing came from about 150 years ago."

One hundred fifty years ago, in my estimation, would have been during the Civil War and I sensed this woman had been in an older historical period than that. There wasn't time in that session to question Judy about this spirit so I just made note of it for the future.

Sure enough, a spirit who was headless returned to Judy and said she was a Queen of England. "This time she told me that whatever the King wanted was granted. She said her husband had beheaded her." So, Judy and I don't know really if this spirit could have been Mary Queen of Scots (the lady dressed in black) or Anne Boleyn, the second wife of Henry VIII, who killed more people than any other king in history. (Author's Note: Actually it was Anne's daughter Elizabeth I who had Mary Queen of Scots killed since it had been proven that Mary had planned Elizabeth's demise so she could become Queen of England.)

"After the spirit is gone I feel tired. When I'm channeling spirits, the synapses I am using in my brain are different than what I use normally to just think. This is what I know so far. I no longer vomit up but now I sometimes get a headache after the reading is over. One thing I like about the good spirits though is that they are quick (Author's Note: See information further on about the perispirit and psychic energy, which are responsible for the thoughts we receive.). Sometimes I get bored with a lot of people because it takes them so long to get to the point but the spirits give me information in lightning speed."

"I had given about ten readings to a couple of my friends and then they had referred a few people because I had been right on with what their dead loved ones had told me. Some of those people continue to call and ask me questions, or some of the spirits of their loved ones keep bothering me to contact the people on Earth. I have kept these contacts going during the time I've been trying to eliminate the imperfect spirits. I just have not taken on any new clients in order to straighten out my situation so I can be more comfortable knowing the difference between the imperfect and good spirits and erase this negativity that was happening in my life."

"It's interesting because I doubted my value as a parent. The good spirits were very sweet and they started giving me affirmations about my parenting. They used to put words in my head like 'You're a good Mom. You look really good.' It was the sweetest thing. It made me not feel so alone and that the world was against me." (Author's Note: We also worked on parenting skills in our therapy).

"That was very nice and then I started to communicate with them. They would ask me questions like when I'd get up at night to eat yogurt. They'd wanted to know what it was. They told me, too, that the drama at my job was put there to keep the people at work busy so no one would think this psychic stuff was going on. Also, they aren't used to a lot of people in the house. I had a friend over last weekend. She happens to be black. So they asked me why I had this person in my house and showed me an old photo of blacks picking cotton in the south. I told them it's different now. She's my friend."

We discussed that spirits have no concept of time and depending on when they died, they would see their world from that vantage point and/or culture. It is our responsibility to teach them what time period and culture they are working with now when they come into our world. (Author's Note: It's interesting that the good spirits were like new friends getting to know Judy and trying to understand her world.)

Animal Magnetism, Hypnosis and Psychological Healing

We feel the force of gravity if we hold two magnets in our hands but we do not see the force itself. Spirits are part of the natural law in humanity. They are everywhere just like gravity. This is how natural law works. Wm. James was known to have said that there is an unseen world all around us. It is important to really *know* this.

Franz Mesmer (1724-1815) believed that a subtle fluid permeated the universe and that all planets influenced the central nervous system in our human bodies through a universally distributed and continuous fluid that ebbed and flowed between the heavenly bodies, Earth and everything on Earth (Kazdin, 2000).

He thought diseases were caused by an imbalance in this fluid. When he applied magnetic passes to a person's body or "laying on of hands" cures of all types of physical and mental illnesses were seen. Many cultures, along with Jesus Christ, practiced this type of healing (Aizpurua, 2013).

Mesmer applied magnet pieces to various parts of a sick person's body as they were laying on a bed and by magnetic passes of his hands he could induce particular trance-like conditions. Sometimes these magnetic influences resulted in cures of such things as blindness, convulsions, paralyses or congestions. He also discovered that the fluid did not work the same on all bodies. His theories were the first step towards the development of hypnotism, psychoanalysis, healing touch and the energizing of water to be used as medicine for the spirit and body (Kazdin, 2000).

Energizing of Water

An example of putting thought energy into water is shown in Masaru Emoto's first book, *The Hidden Messages in Water* (2004), which shows photographs of each pattern of crystals that are formed when water crystallized and recorded the essence of the water in a Petri dish. Some dishes of water were spoken to, some were prayed over, some had music played to them, etc. The photographs of these different crystallizations are fascinating (Photos begin on p. 7).

One of Emoto's main points of this book was that as babies we are made of over 90% of water and now as older adults at least 70% water is contained in our bodies. So, if the water is affected by words or pictures shown to it, we are also affected by words, images and thoughts because of the water inside of us.

Another point he stresses is if the "frequency" is wrong in your life or with the water, you can correct that frequency by sending love to the water or the person. He stated, "Words have their individual and unique vibrational frequencies" (Emoto, 2004, p. 142). One of the themes of his book is the power of intention and the power of affirmation/s. And, "No matter what your intentions, announcing them is an important step" (Emoto, 2004, p. 141).

The Universal Cosmic Fluid (or Psychic Energy)— The Primitive Element in Matter

As stated above, the universal cosmic fluid (see *perispirit* below) is a basic and primitive element in matter. The results of this fluid are found in nature. "Etherization and imponderability (the normal primitive state)" (Kardec, (2009), p. 354) are the two states of this fluid. The dictionary states that etherization is the act of administering ether and the person then comes under its influence. The dictionary also states that imponderability is something that cannot be weighed or measured. This word imponderability was used formerly to designate heat, light, electricity and magnetism and then was a term applied to ether or to spiritual or mental phenomena.

Heat, light, electricity and magnetism are terms which come under the jurisdiction of science and the material world. It has been said that the job of science is to learn and understand natural laws. Spiritual phenomena come under the jurisdiction of the unseen world that William James speaks about. The fluid spiritual element of the *perispirit* cannot be detected by our scientific instruments.

A client of mine who is an engineer simply stated the following facts one evening upon leaving my office. "Physics has always been looking for unifying theories and one of the things they've come up with and have started to demonstrate is something called 'dark matter.' They believe that this is the sort of thing that holds things together." (Author's Note: As in Mesmer's magnetism or the Spiritist *perispirit*—see explanation below—or the concept of psychic energy.*)

Magnetism and electricity are related to one another. This may also be a way we could channel into one another, as in telepathy. It's called induction which is an entrance or an initiation. For instance, in speaking of electricity, the flow of movement of electrons is what induces a magnetic flow. The metal that's in the magnet has a structure that allows the electrons to flow in a freer way than it does in other elements.

The electrons in the magnet or in an electrical wire hit a resonance, which in physics is the reinforced vibration of a body exposed to the vibration at about the same frequency." And, the medium in receiving this magnetic charge from the spirits acts as an induction bridge which is a form of balance that measures the value of electric resistances.

Judy states that her vibration has gotten higher since she first felt the negative spirits in her house. One thing she does to raise her vibrational level is to read spiritual literature. She has also gotten used to the good spirits who give her information. At one time she would vomit after receiving information from them. Now she sometimes just gets a headache. So her vibration over all has become higher, also, because she now understands the process of mediumship and the natural laws that govern it.

Now, if a spirit shows itself in front of her, she can decide, "Is this a good or a bad spirit?" She may send a thought "Where are you from?" If they don't answer her, she ignores them. If they have more positive energy, they will at least say hello or introduce themselves. She is helping them to come in and/or acting as an induction bridge.

Magnetism and electricity are related to one another, which is another reason that spirits or ghosts "come in" on phone wires, computer screens, televisions, electrical lights, etc. If they try to show themselves to us, we feel the force of them maybe because the electrical lights in the room have just gone on and off. Since it's an unseen force we need to understand how psychic energy or the *perispirit* works.

You may want to put two magnets of equal size four to six inches apart from each other on your kitchen counter and push them closer and closer to each other. Soon they will BANG together. You didn't see the unseen force of magnetism but you saw the result. They are now attached to each other.

Psychic phenomena work this way in attracting spiritual direction or information to all of us that our guiding spirits, angels and/or positive ancestors think we need at the moment. One problem in our receiving of this information is that we often are not paying attention to information from the unseen world.

Spiritists' Philosophy

Spiritists' philosophy has named this fluid body of the soul the *perispirit* (Kardec, 2009, p. 47). They believe it is inseparable from the soul and is one of the forming elements in the making of a human being. Most importantly, it is the means by which thought is transmitted. The perispirit is responsible for all psychic phenomena , which rest on the natural laws of the universe (Aizpurua, 2013, p. 95). The nature of the perispirit is affected by the degree of morality of the spirit.

During our physical life, the perispirit is the connection between spirit and matter and it is connected to our physiological and psychological make-up. Since the perispirit is the way in which thought is transmitted, it is responsible for connecting spirit and our material world, which then makes it responsible for all paranormal and spiritual phenomena (Kardec, 2009, p. 47).

Thought Communication Bridges Time and Space

This fluid condenses around the focal point of intelligence or the soul and, as stated above, it is the means of how thought is transmitted. This thought communication is what bridges time and space. It is the natural aspect of how we exist. Perhaps the most important point from a Spiritists' perspective is that nature is all around us. God has created nature, and its forces act mechanically. We know this because nature keeps happening over and over again.

The Spiritists state that when we see nature, we need to know that there is a God who created it. According to their theory, nature is our proof that there is a God. All of nature is immersed in the *perispirit* and we are part of nature. This forming element that creates human beings acts like ether and we come under its influence. Just as we understand nature, we need to understand that *perispirit*, which like magnetism and electricity is a force that is also unseen. "It is revealed to us in intentional, premeditated and calculated acts which is an exclusive attribute of the soul" (Kardec, 2009, p. 101). Our soul is normally invisible to us; however, it is the highest center of wisdom and perspective. The acts of the soul, which are aided by spirits are everywhere; but, like gravity, magnetism and electricity, we cannot see the force of the soul itself. We become awakened to God and spirits through happenings in our lives, and we become awakened to our soul when we die.

Types of Universes

According to Barham & Greene (1986) in their book *The Silver Cord Lifeline to the Unobstructed,* there are three universes that affect us constantly. One is the physical universe that we live in, the other is the unobstructed universe where our soul goes between and after our lives (Author's Note: Imperfect spirits live here.) and lastly is the universe of God or the universal intelligence.

The biggest difference is the frequency at which energy functions in these three areas. (Author's Note: Remember that Judy was reading inspirational literature in order to raise her frequency.) Barham and Greene stress that these three energies are always functioning interdependently and that psychic energy permeates all three universes and is used as a communication link between them. This book also states that there is a silver cord that connects our soul to our body which is not broken until we die. (Author's Note: Psychic energy would include the Spiritists *perispirit*.)

A spirit's normal life is one of freedom which is why we fly away at night when we sleep. (Author's Note: And the silver cord keeps us attached to our body so we can return to it after our journeying at night when we dream or whenever we leave our bodies.) It is also why our soul really becomes alive when we die so we can return to the universe of God. It is the soul that takes on the ethereal body and becomes a ghost.

The Spiritists believe that our *perispirit* (like the silver cord) holds your spirit to your body. It is broken only at the time of death. Your soul may leave your body but it will come back when its presence is needed. Remember that your spiritual guides give you intuitions that suggest new ideas and thoughts to you justifying what Freud and Jung called the unconscious.

When Freud defended the idea of the unconscious during his Ph.D. dissertation, he told his committee that people wrote down questions before they went to bed and then were given answers while they slept. He said the answers came from their unconscious. It seems he only had one-half of the formula.

If he had listened to Carl Jung, he would have understood that the bottom layer of our unconscious contains our soul and from this spiritual element of our unconscious come our answers in life. Mostly this must be because we come into this life with a plan and our soul knows what that plan is before we enter our mother's womb.

The trance-like states that Mesmer brought forth were regarded as altered states of consciousness which led to the understanding sixty years later of hypnosis (James Braid, 1795-1860). Mesmer's teaching of induced trances helped people to begin to make contact with spirits.

After Mesmer, Sigmund Freud was exposed to hypnosis through the work of Jean-Martin Charcot (1825-1893) and he used it for a period of time. Paracelsus (1493-1541), a distinguished Swiss physician whom Carl Jung (1875-1961) studied, believed that we attracted astral fluids which nourished our soul and that we could also heal others through the use of these fluids. Carl Jung believed we needed to get to know our soul before we could live life fully. Jung mentions in "The Symbolic Life" (Vol. 18 of his *Collected Works*, para. 797) that the art of "Mesmerism" accomplished much good. He stated that Mesmer imitated many miraculous cures of priests and of those found by people on a pilgrimage to religious places.

Your Soul Is Developed From Your Life Story

Your soul begins to become visible during your life when you sometimes realize you have extrasensory or synchronistic experiences. Spirits send images and flashes of inspiration to you through your soul. Your will also deepens with the crises of everyday life when you are looking for answers to what is happening to you. One starts to realize that there is a spirit part that *knows*. These "Ah Ha" moments let us have a glimpse of our soul even if we don't realize it at the time.

When We "Die" Our Soul Comes "Alive"

We usually connect to our soul when we are so-called "dead" (Stead, 1910, p. 16). The soul leaves your body out of the top of your head. Your body then looks wispy and contains your mind and soul. Leaving your body is like shedding your skin or peeling a banana. Your body is simply the vehicle, like a car, that aids in your soul's growth here on Earth.

There is a plan for your life only it isn't necessarily the one you have mapped out in your mind. A Higher Power is guiding you to meet the angels who have been sent to you as friends, relatives, meaningful relationships, etc. You need faith and belief in this process as you remember that one-half of life is just showing up.

Client's Life - Dysfunctional and Difficult (Normal is that 95% of our Population is Dysfunctional)

Judy told me many things about her childhood and family of origin. In one session she stated the following:

> I don't speak to my family members anymore. They like to insult me. They think I'm the stupid, dumb one. Everybody has to be the same in my family. It's mediocrity that they really want. My father is always talking about how bright he is. I want to say to him, "Dude, you've been arrested and in jail several times. What's so brilliant about that?"

> My brother Jimmy is so smart that he's 40 years old and living with my mother. And, my mother was "gaslighting" me all the time. (Author's Note: See *Gaslight, a* 1944 movie.) My mother is very passive, and she says things very sweetly most of the time. She would constantly say to me, "Oh, honey, is that what you thought? You must have misinterpreted what I said to you." And she was the one who didn't drink!

> She would spread vicious rumors about me so the other relatives would stay away from me. Her sweetness was so she didn't have to admit the cruelty that was happening in our home. Our father was drunk and beating up my brothers. She wouldn't look at what was happening because if she did she'd have to get a divorce

and a job. She didn't want to have to leave the house.
This hell was what she chose for all of us as a result.

No wonder I drank and did drugs when I left home. It
was so chaotic there. My grandmother's spirit has come
in recently and told me that my father incested my
brothers. I always knew that there was this "stuff" going
on that I just couldn't put together. I felt "crazy" there a
lot and it was always my fault because I must be
misunderstanding something."

I know now that the angry one in the family knows
there's some kind of sham going on in their family and
they say so. Then because they are stating the truth, they
become the angry one—the problem child—the difficult
one. They, the problem child, becomes a threat to the
family so the family then wants to discredit this child.

Whether you are the hero, the scapegoat, the quiet one, or the mascot
of your family, your soul comes to Earth to learn and is developed from
your life story. Your soul contains your possibilities, your talents and
your unrealized potential. It also contains your personality, your
imagination and your intelligence along with your past, present and
future. In describing her journey into her psychic ability, we can see
how her unrealized potential was hidden from her.

Judy's soul contained a great deal of intelligence but like many
people it took her years to develop this knowledge, and then when it
seemed as if she couldn't take it a minute longer, she started to pray for
help. How confusing it must have seemed when that help was
sometimes good information from good spirits but the negative ones kept
interfering.

The Internet Saves the Day

"When I was seeing all these negative spirits, I got on the Internet so
fast and started just plugging in words that were happening to me. I was
lead to all these articles and You Tube videos which eventually got me to
my medium coach and then to you. Once I wrote down your name, my
good guides told me that you were going to be instrumental in
developing this aspect of my life. They said that you are respected and
that you have helped a lot of people."

After Judy had seen me for a few sessions, she stated, "I wish
someone had told me about William James and Carl Jung when these
first things had started to happen to me. One thing I don't understand: if

seeing spirits, whether they are imperfect or good, is supposed to be a spiritual experience, what is so spiritual about it if I feel crazy?" I told her what she had felt was a spiritual emergency (Grof, 1989). "Yes, that's what mine was! An emergency! I wish more people knew about this psychology of yours. A lot of people would feel less 'crazy.'"

"Before my twelve-step programs, I was not a happy person. I had these thought patterns that were placed in me by my negative mother. I had to cut out those negative thoughts just like a cancer. I also believed I had to suffer and that life had to be difficult. I know now that's not true. It doesn't mean there's not effort involved or consistency. There is. However, we all need to listen to what gives us the most joy and do those things too."

It's very important for a therapist to acknowledge the work a client has already done, whether in other therapies or in self-help programs. I did this with Judy and stressed that her work in our sessions and the homework involved outside of the sessions would be the most helpful for her. For those of you who are not familiar with twelve-step programs, there will be a list of a few of them on the bibliography that may be helpful to you.

People who are working a twelve-step recovery program believe in giving back. Once they achieve quality sobriety, they will pick people up to drive them to and from meetings, run meetings on either the twelve steps of their program or on certain themes such as anger, shame, relationships, codependency, etc. In this service work, they display the gratitude for those who have helped them and are able to give back to others.

Below are the original twelve-steps as published by Alcoholics Anonymous (A.A. World Services, Inc., 2001). The spiritual aspects of the program can be seen from the steps which are:

- "Came to believe that a power greater than ourselves could restore us to sanity.
- Made a decision to turn our will and our lives over to the care of God as we understood Him.
- Admitted to God, to ourselves, and to another human being, the exact nature of our wrongs.
- Humbly asked Him to remove our shortcomings (Author's Note: So prayer is important).
- Sought through prayer and meditation to improve our conscious contact with God as we understood Him, praying only for knowledge of His will for us and the power to carry that out.

- Having had a spiritual awakening as the result of these steps, we tried to carry this message to alcoholics and to practice these principles in all our affairs (A.A., 2001, Chapter 5).

Most other twelve-step recovery meetings are patterned after the A.A. model. There are different types of groups such as: Debtors Anonymous, Incest Anonymous, Overeaters Anonymous, Narcotics Anonymous, etc. There is usually a table with pamphlets and reading material at every meeting that are either free or sold at a minimal cost. If you are curious about these meetings, anyone can attend an Open (O) meeting.

Other types of meetings are Speaker (S) meetings, BB (Big Book) meetings, Step (S) meetings, Discussion (D) meetings and Beginners (B) meetings. A list of meetings in your area can be obtained from the Internet. Meetings are now held all over the world. When you attend meetings don't be shy about asking questions about what you don't understand. However, remember Bill Wilson's adage about meetings which is also a good rule for life. He is known to have said, "Take what you need and leave the rest." In other words, be discerning and try to be with the people there who have some of the same values as you have.

Our job on Earth is to develop trust and intuition. These meetings consistently helped Judy to be with honest people who were working to improve their lives just as she was. Confusion usually means you are working through something and new opportunities are awaiting you. Be curious during your confusion.

Judy has certainly been able to persist through her confusion, which is a positive trait that comes when a person is raised in confusion in the first place. Another job on your journey called life is to go beyond your ego. Your ego is everything you would say after "I am...." Your ego says we have no spiritual guides and there is no unseen world. Your ego doesn't know everything. Thanks to the Internet and reading material, Judy educated her ego.

Another purpose of your soul is to make you human. As you address and overcome pain and frustration you will connect to who you really are. Pain opens you to other dimensions. Hurt people mistreat other people in order to get even. They create their own karma and learn their lessons in this way. Remember, along with learning our own lessons, we come to Earth to play a part in the drama of others' lessons as well.

Drama people are the type who are complaining and mentioning what happened twenty years ago and trying to punish people for that. They are not usually satisfied with their life and would be considered by many to be "high maintenance." Drama has identity. They need this drama because they don't know who they are yet, so they haven't fully matured and maybe never will. They feel persecuted in life and the persecutor position has the power of being "right." They sometimes have many degrees of anger because of feeling righteous or martyred, which eventually leads to hateful feelings. Perpetrators of harm to others will do penance by setting themselves up as victims of this harm in their next life.

Because Judy attended almost ten years of different types of twelve-step meetings, her anger was greatly reduced, her self-esteem had improved, she was learning how to have real friends who she cared for and they cared for her. She had a better body image and was sincerely working on lowering her weight even more than she had; and mostly, she just felt safer in the world as a result of her work in the recovery rooms.

Being in Crisis Sometimes Leads to a Spiritual Experience or Emergency

It's interesting to note that both Judy and Bill Wilson, a founder of A.A., had been on their knees in crisis asking God for help, which created their spiritual awakenings. Bill Wilson did not believe there was a God but he prayed in a hospital room one night, "If there is a God, please take away my desire to drink." His spiritual experience was light that filled the room and his desire to drink was gone.

His story can be read in *Alcoholics Anonymous,* (2001), a book that is known as the "Blue Book," because of its color. The Blue Book, published in 1939, contains stories of approximately one-hundred first-time members of A.A. and is very inspirational for alcoholics and their family members to read. (Author's Note: For family member's education, please attend Alanon meetings to better understand how you can help and stop enabling the alcoholic. (See Bibliography for Internet address.)

Spirituality is the experience of the spirit and both Bill and Judy received it in different ways in order to fit into their lives. Bill Wilson's spiritual experience had some characteristics of a typical experience such as a transient, extraordinary experience marked by feelings of unity, harmonious relationship to the divine and everything in existence as well as euphoric feelings and the sense of lacking control over the event (Herrick, 2008).

Judy's, too, includes a sense of union with the positive spirits and it is giving her a great sense of meaning and purpose in her life. This is what William James said happened with a spiritual experience, which began with a need for help and ended with a sense that the person had been helped. Once a person eventually understands and incorporates their spiritual experience into their life, they have an increased appreciation for life and live with more spiritual values toward all. Eyes are the windows to the soul. This physical attribute has more impact when soul mates meet here on Earth than any other. There is a familiarity when you meet a soul mate—a *knowing*. You are supposed to mature based on overcoming your many difficult body assignments during your task-oriented life or lives.

All souls are held accountable for their conduct in the bodies they occupy. Sometimes meeting a soul mate if one is already married causes a difficult assignment on Earth because one has to choose using the values they've received from their family-of-origin or their culture, but feeling the pull of a *knowing* that very few people around them can understand is sometimes unbearable.

Carl Jung, during a crisis-oriented time in his life spoke to his soul. "My soul where are you? Do you hear me? I speak. I call you—are you there? I have returned. I am here again…One thing you must *know*; the one thing I have learned is that one must live this life" (Shamdasani, 2009, p. 232). Sometimes living this life can cause one to have to make very difficult choices. Since Judy has discovered her psychic abilities, spirits now help her make better decisions.

Getting Information from Spirits

Judy explains what it's like to live with her good and pure spirits. "Regarding psychic information, I ask for specific things and then I don't get any response. Other times I do. I could just be thinking in my mind about something (Author's Note: This is how spirits communicate with us all. They give us certain thoughts using the *perispirit* and/or psychic energy.) It isn't up to me which responses I get. I can't control which information comes to me. I can ask for it but it doesn't mean I get the specific thing I want."

This little voice in our head sometimes comes from spirits and at another time could come from our unconscious hangover from childhood which could be negative and about to create some type of drama. We, as Judy did, need to be discerning about what we listen to and take action on.

Judy now states,

The psychic information just comes as an idea. The closest human concept I can give you is that the energy changes. It doesn't affect me at all now. A thought in my head doesn't exhaust me. Spirit guides don't take any energy exchange. They initiate a lot of stuff. They put ideas into my head. 'Go pay this bill. You forgot to fill out that form.' Or they will warn me about things. For instance, someone at work was saying something to me the other day and a picture of a snake came into my head. The snake would repeat the hissing while this woman was talking. I knew not to trust what she was telling me.

I also, in my mind, shot light from my eyes and hands. The light would come out at 100 pixels which I would direct toward the negative spirits. The negative image would leave completely. The more I was able to dismiss them or cut them up, the stronger I felt. Now I don't think about them that much anymore.

I also imagined there were angels around my doors and window. They were trying to tell me they were protecting me. The image of them trying to protect me made me feel safe. So, in my mind, I now think that I am safe and I am being protected. If people feel like they are victims they become victims because what they think, they create. We are all creating our own reality.

When I asked Judy why she believed the spirits had chosen her, she stated: "Because I'm honest, I've suffered a lot, done some recovery work and they know I'm not about trying to manipulate anyone or force an outcome. They trust that I won't use this energy for devious purposes. They just keep showing a silhouette of me and I'm clear. They say that I'm humble and I don't brag about this 'gift' that I've received." (Author's Note: This is one difference between a spiritual experience and mental illness—that the spiritual experience makes one humble while a hallucination causes the person to act in a grandiose manner. The mentally ill person also cannot tell you the same story over and over again as the spiritual person can. For more information on the differences between mental illness and spiritual experiences, please see ASCS (2014), pp. 213-214.

"They say people are going to trust me and that people need someone to trust. They can also get to me and have sometimes when I've said I don't want to do this. They know that I'm interested in helping people who are still alive to ease their pain. That really gets to me and they know it because I know what it's like to be in pain. I'm in a transition now. I feel as if I'm in a hallway and I want to get to this new life quickly. Sometimes this middle ground just feels like it's too much."

We both agreed that the waiting time in life sometimes seems as if it takes too long. However, the spirit world has been known to say that this waiting time helps us really understand what it is each individual is supposed to learn.

"What I'm only starting to become aware of is that you can choose your own destiny to some extent. I can now see why I was so different from my family. I do want to help others. Because I've been in twelve-step programs, just being exposed to people who are genuinely nice to me has affected me. It's validating to me that there was something wrong in my family and I knew it. My family can't stop good things from happening to me anymore. The worst is over and there's a reason my pain had to be so deep. I hope I can teach people that one of the problems in their lives is their belief system. You have to believe you are entitled to good things and then you will receive them."

Another thing both Judy and I know is that we need all of you to spread the word—to help develop a consensus that there are spiritual guides for us all who are helping us. It's important to tell your spiritual experience that you've kept to yourself for fear of being labeled crazy to some other people you can trust. The spirits will probably clap when you do that as Judy told me one day during a session "The guides are all clapping because we said we *know* they are there helping us all."

The Soul After So-Called Death

"When the soul leaves the body it remains exactly the same as when it was in the body; the soul, which is the only real self, and which uses the mind and the body as its instruments, no longer has the use or the need of the body. But it retains the mind, knowledge, experience, the habits of thought, the inclinations; they remain exactly as they were…the real self is liberated by death" (Stead, 1910, p. 21).

If one watches television in the United States, it is filled with what is known as the "supernatural" (Author's Note: From reading this paper I hope you now know that spirits are natural.). Some of the shows are entitled "Salem," "The Walking Dead," "American Horror Story," "Penny Dreadful," etc. These shows all bring to us the belief that fear of the dark, the unknown and fear of spirits is normal. At least equal time could be given to the work of the good spirits who want to help people and who do just that.

Judy mentioned that her family was really not interested in change—that they wanted to stay mediocre. She reminded me of something I remember that Abraham Maslow (1963) wrote: "The greatest cause of our alienation from our real selves is our neurotic involvements with other people, the historical hangovers from childhood, and the irrational transferences, in which past and present are confused. And in which the adult acts like a child" (p. 7). Scotton, Chinen & Battista (1996) continued with…From this perspective, culture can be seen…as a shared conspiracy against self-knowledge and psychological growth in which people collude to protect one another's defenses and illusions" (p. 400).

I hope Judy and I have helped you understand that spirits are just people who have discarded their bodies. Just like there are negative people, there are negative spirits and they can be sent away. For the most part, what Judy's story has shown me is how helpful and kind they can be and how hard they work so people will not stay mediocre or stuck in their hangovers from childhood. As we help to develop a consensus that spirit phenomena can and does happen, we also need to realize that most spirits just want to guide us for our soul development using the natural laws that were given to them by infinite intelligence.

Bibliography

A.A. World Services, Inc. (Ed.). (2001). *Alcoholics Anonymous* (4th Ed.). NY: AA World Services, Inc.

Alcoholics-Anonymous. www.alcoholics-anonymous.org. Al-anon, Alateen. www.al-anon.alateen.org

Aizpurua, Jon (2013). *Fundamentals of Spiritism.* (Translation of Epsilon Book S.R.L., 2000)

Association for Research & Enlightenment. www.edgarcayce.org/

Barhan, Martha J., R.N., Ph.D. & Greene, James T., Ph.D.. (1986). *The Silver Cord Lifeline to the Unobstructed.* CA: DeVorss & Co.

Emoto, M. (2004). *The Hidden Messages in Water.* (D.A. Thayne, Trans.). OR: Beyond Words Publishing

Gaslight (1944 movie). Produced by Arthur Hornblow, Jr. Metro-Goldwyn-Mayer. (Ingrid Bergman and Charles Boyer in starring roles).

Grof, S., M.D. & Grof, C. (1989). *Spiritual Emergency When Personal Transformation Becomes a Crisis.* CA: Jeremy P. Tarcher Inc.

Herrick, Karen Ph.D. (2006/2011). *You're Not Finished Yet.* IN: Author House

Herrick, Karen Ph.D. (2008). *Naming Spiritual Experiences* (Thesis). MI: ProQuest Information and Learning Company. http://gateway.proquest.com/openurl?url_ver=Z39.88-2004&res_dat=xri:pqdiss&rft_val_fmt=info:ofi/fmt:kev:mtx:dissertation&rft_dat=xri:pqdiss:3299617

Hogan, R. Craig, Ph.D. (Ed.) (2014). *Afterlife Communication—16 Proven Methods, 85 True Accounts.* Chapter 12 Herrick:

"Understanding Afterlife and Angel Contacts." (Pgs. 211-228). IL: Greater Reality Publications

James, William/Wikipedia: www.pbs.org/wgbh/.../william_bio.html

Jung, C. G. (1969) "The Symbolic Life Miscellaneous Writings. *Collected Works* (Vol. 18, pp. 797). Bollinger Series XX. NJ: Princeton University Press.

Jung, C.G. (2009) (Edited by Sonu Shamdasani). *The Red Book Liber Novus*. NY: W.W. Norton & Co.

Kardec, Allan (2009). *GENESIS Miracles and Predictions According to Spiritism*. Brazil: International Spiritist Council

Kazdin, Alan E. (2000). *Encyclopedia of Psychology*. NY: Oxford University Press, Vol.5, Learni to Opposi for Mesmer, Franz

Limoges, Yvonne, Director & Editor, Spiritist Society of Florida (Est. 1982), St. Petersburg, Fl. ylimoges@aol.com Personal Conversation (2014)

Maslow, A.H. (1963). "The Creative Attitude." *The Structurist*, pgs. 4-10.

Newton, Michael, Ph.D. (1994/2013). *Journey of Souls Case Studies of Life Between Lives*. MINN: Llewellyn Publications

Scotton, B. W., M.D, Chinen, A, B, M.D., & Battista, J.R,M.D.(Eds.), (1996). Textbook of Transpersonal Psychiatry and Psychology. NY: Basic Books.

Shamdasani, Sonu, Ed. (1990). *The Red Book Liber Novus C.G. Jung*. NY: WW Norton & Co.

Stead, W.T. (1910). *Letters from Julia*. Ill: The Progressive Thinker Publishing House (p. 16).

Biography

Rev. Karen E. Herrick, Ph.D., LCSW, LMSW, CADC, is the director of the Center for Children of Alcoholics, Inc., in Red Bank, New Jersey. After finishing her master's degree in social work from Rutgers University, she began to educate families on the disease concept of alcoholism. She developed a successful private practice, eventually seeing all types of people with psychological problems, including addictions.

Her book, *You're Not Finished Yet,* encapsulates her private practice work. The book includes two chapters on spirituality and spiritual experiences inspired by her Holy Spirit experience during holotropic breathwork training.

She attended more educational sessions in California through the Spiritual Emergence Network, and eventually completed a Ph.D. at the Union Institute & University in Cincinnati, Ohio. Her thesis was entitled

Naming Spiritual Experiences. Of the 133 mental health professionals she researched, 75% stated that they believed further education about spiritual experiences, near-death experiences (NDEs) and/or after-life experiences would be beneficial to them personally and professionally. During her therapeutic practice, she encourages some clients to visit with mediums to aid in handling their grief and loss of loved ones.

She was ordained at the Cathedral of St. John the Divine and uses her Interfaith ministry to be actively involved in using the Spiritual Psychology of William James, Carl Jung, and Abraham Maslow with clients and people everywhere. She is presently the first female president in thirty-seven years of the Academy for Spiritual and Consciousness Studies (ASCS). She has recently completed requirements for certification with the American Center for Integration of Spiritually Transformative Experiences (ACISTE). The mental health professionals she researched indicated they needed more networking opportunities. One of her purposes now is to educate these professionals by first welcoming them into the ASCS organization as members.

Karen has shared her clinical expertise for twenty-seven years in her private practice by lecturing throughout the United States on dysfunctional and addictive homes, dissociation, grief and loss from a Jungian perspective. From this perspective, she has discovered that visits to mediums greatly help people in chronic grief to continue with their lives.

Karen is available for private therapy in her office, on Skype and Face Time. She can be reached at www.karenherrick.com or 732 530-8513. Her new web site is www.spiritualexperiences.info. She is interested in hearing about your spiritual experiences.

Receiving and Understanding Signs

Joe Higgins

Abstract

This paper contains descriptions of how people can receive
and understand the signs that their loved ones in spirit are
around them and anxious to communicate. It explains how the
process of giving and receiving signs actually works and the
most commonly experienced signs. It then describes why those
on the other side of life come to us and answers these questions:
"Can I ask for a sign?" "Why don't I get a sign?" "How do we
know it's an authentic sign?" "Is there any way I can increase
my chances of getting a sign?"

Receiving and Understanding Signs

By Joseph M Higgins

In this article, I describe how to receive and understand signs from
our departed loved ones.

I've been able to sense others around me since I was a young child. I
spent many nights wide awake between midnight and three o'clock in the
morning trying to make sense of the activities that were going around in
my room. I felt different presences, I saw orbs, which are like balls of
light, and actually felt physical phenomenon, such as someone touching
my hand or sitting on my bed.

Now back then no one really talked about this type of activity. This
type of subject would come up rarely, and if it did it was usually late at
night between adults after they've had a few drinks.

But nowadays people are much more open to the possibilities of this phenomena. More people come forward and talk about their interaction with the spirit side of life. Granted, many people still look at you like you have two heads, but it is much easier to talk about these types of activities today than it was 40 years ago.

As I grew up I kept this information to myself and people thought I was just "sensitive." Once I got into high school I started to mention some of the things that happened to me to some close friends and slowly I began to come out of my shell.

At this point in my life there was still some activity when I tried to go to sleep at night. But after working all day and perhaps being out with my friends at night the last thing I wanted to do was deal with some type of circus when I wanted to sleep. So my attitude became "do whatever you want but keep it down. I have to work in the morning"

Fast-forward 15 years. Continuing to read and ask questions about the afterlife, I decided to try to get real answers about the things that I had experienced.

After being introduced to others that had "special gifts" I did not feel so isolated and alone. Here were people who had the same experiences as I had, and we were able to talk and discuss various aspects of it.

I joined a development circle to increase my awareness and sensitivity and to learn the process of mediumship. Some people have a natural ability from day one. But most of us must learn techniques to increase our connection and to protect ourselves. There's so much that goes into mediumship but we are not going to get into that today because that in itself is a whole different presentation and I'll leave that to some of our other experts here with us this weekend.

So, what I'd like to do today is go over some general understanding on how the process works of giving a sign, receiving a sign and understanding a sign.

We'll look at it from soup to nuts, as they say. Often, people think that signs are created after a loved one passes. But actually the information that they'll use is created while they are still alive.

So I'll explain about how the actual process works.

I'll also explain different popular signs. These are the signs that are most often sent and received and understood. They do try to keep it simple, because a lot of times we are not the sharpest tacks in the box.

I will explain why they even come to us. What's their motivation, what's their reason?

I'll try to answer some of the most common questions that all of us have about signs, such as

- Can I ask for sign?

- Why don't I get a sign?
- How do we know it's an authentic sign?
- Is there any way I can increase my chances of getting a sign?

According to recent polls, over 20 million people have felt as if they had received a sign from someone on the other side. How many people in the past have received a sign? We'll never know. But with today's technology polling techniques, the willingness to be more open about this type of subject we can get a pretty good understanding of how many people have had some type of interaction. Now that number is just in America and does not include other countries.

It also doesn't include people who believe that this can happen but it has never happened to them personally.

For clinicians, your clients might have experienced some of these signs and are reluctant to talk about them for fear that you might think that they are crazy. But remember that it's not uncommon for this to happen. If you've had an experience, you are among millions who have had similar contact. You will have it if you want to.

I add "if you want to" because some people accept the process and the belief that it's possible but don't want to be contacted for various reasons. We'll go over some of those reasons when we talk about the process and how everything works.

How the Process Actually Works

The first step is what I call the Evaluation Period.

This is the timeframe after a loved one passes when certain decisions are made. Some of the decisions that have to be made are

- will a sign be given, if at all
- how it will be done
- when it will be done
- where it will be done

When a loved one crosses over, they go through a stage of acclimating to the new environment. There are guides and teachers who will help them with the communication process if a sign is determined to be sent.

So they will evaluate the situation at hand. They will decide if it is the right time, and who might be best to receive a sign.

An initial sign or even signs at any time may not be given due to various reasons such as the following:

Religious beliefs. I've had people tell me that they believe in signs but that their religion does not allow it. So they are reluctant to ask & accept a sign.

People are too distraught. They may be in the middle of the grieving process and any attempt at sending a sign may cause more harm and confusion. If it is believed that a sign would bring discomfort it would be delayed or even not allowed to happen at all.

At times individuals who have passed will be so anxious to send a sign that they will not obey the guidelines and attempt to send the sign on their own. Frequently this ends up scaring or confusing the recipient.

Once the decision has been made (by the individual, teachers and guides) that the sign will be sent, they must decide how it will be done. This process will begin with evaluating the deceased loved ones entire life and coordinating certain memories that are associated with themselves and to the person who will received a sign.

So what happens is it's like walking down the aisle in the supermarket. And all the products on all the shelves are different parts of your life. One might be a birthday, honeymoon, favorite food, one of the cars you had owned that was a favorite of yours, things like this. So they will take a particular memory that is associated with your loved one and use that as a possible sign to send to you.

An example of this might be someone who loved fishing. They had all the special equipment they read all the books, and they shared their joy of fishing with those around them. When a sign from them comes through there is a good chance it might be associated with something to do with fishing. But if this particular person had no interest in say horse racing, they're not going to send you a sign about a horse race. Unless of course you're at the races and one of the horses name is "Dad's Gone Fishing." Then that's probably a sign for you.

So they are going to use something that is familiar to you about them.

Another question that must be answered is **where it will be done**. This can also be of use, because memories of certain places are very important to us. Some of us love the beach, others love the desert, some people like to go to the movies etc. So if you're in that environment and the thought of a loved one comes to you, there is a greater chance they were using the actual place as a stepping stone to get your attention.

And one of the main questions is **when will it be done**. Sometimes signs are sent right after passing. This could be due to your total focus around the individual. Your attention is not taken away by outside stimulus like weekly TV shows, things at work, the daily drama that usually surrounds our lives. So it's easier for them to get a sign through right away.

However it's a double-edged sword. It also can be the hardest time to get a sign. People are emotionally upset; they're anxious; they can be tired and stressed. A sign can be met with confusion and cause additional anxiety and misunderstanding. So they will hold off and try at a later time.

Sometimes they come through other family members or even friends, because they know the family members or friends will pass this information on to you at the proper time. This is not uncommon. It has happened in my own life and possibly yours.

One of the techniques to increase your ability to receive a sign is the ability to put yourself in a relaxed state of mind. Meditation is one of the best ways to open up the communication highway to make contact. And there are a lot of great teachers here this weekend who could help you with this. But for the average Joe, I like to tell them to be aware of the times when a sign may come through.

Some of these times are at night when you're sleeping. Dreams are the number one way for our loved ones to contact us. We are more relaxed, they have access to memory processing configuration, and they can use visuals much more easily.

I also found that daydreaming is a perfect way for them to access you while you're awake. Other forms of meditation that can be done besides the ones in which you sit in silence:

- Some people like to garden.
- Some people like to listen to music.
- Some people like to read.
- Some people like to paint.

Or anything else that relaxes you to outside stimulus. In sports they call it being in the zone meaning you're very focused and you have the ability to shut down outside stimulus.

So the everyday person can also set up the atmosphere of being able to be contacted not only through meditation, but also by participating in a hobby or action that they can feel like they can get lost in.

With these types of activities you will increase the chances of communication at a higher level, perhaps even hearing sentences which could develop into conversations.

Types of Signs That Are Commonly Used

We talked about dreams.

This is a no-brainer, no pun intended, for the ease of access to us.

Different smells and scents are a very common sign.

When my dad comes to me I can smell cigars.

Some people report smelling perfume, cologne, flowers, cigarette smell and even coffee. One time when my mom came through, the whole room filled up with the smell of fresh-brewed coffee. And toward the end of her life that is one of the few things she really enjoyed.

Another way is through electricity manipulation

Lights going on and off, radios turning on, hearing certain songs, or even hairdryers turning on can be signs.

Hairdryer Story

On the night that we had the wake for my mother, my sister returned home tired and went directly to bed. We had a long day the next day and she wanted to grab some sleep. About two o'clock in the morning she woke up to a loud noise in the bathroom. She couldn't understand what it could be, so she got up and went to see what was happening. Her hair dryer was plugged in and turned on full blast. She knew right away it was a sign from our mother. She had no intention of washing and setting her hair at 11 o'clock at night and then going to bed. She had planned to do this first thing in the morning and so the sign came through loud and clear.

Sounds and Music

Many times people will be thinking of their loved ones and their favorite song will come on the radio. Most of the time we believe that they have manipulated that particular song to play at that particular moment. And yes, they can do that. But from what I've learned, they know that particular song is going to be played at that particular time and then they push the thought of themselves into our minds. So they get us thinking about them, and we think it's our action of thinking about them. Tricky, aren't they? Hey, whichever way they use, it works.

Sometimes we could hear them actually calling our name. This is also not uncommon. And the interesting thing here is that they use their own inflection so we recognize who it is. Sometimes we're not sure who it is because we've been distracted by other things going on at the same time. But they can use other common sounds.

They also use some other very common signs, such as the following.

Coins

When people tell stories about finding certain **coins** over and over they can relate to it because the chances are they've heard others tell similar stories.

Many people have heard stories of people finding coins, pennies or dimes that are associated with the deceased loved one.

I have witnessed this with my girlfriend finding quarters everywhere. It seems to runs in streaks. A couple of years ago, we were finding them every day. And I always like to say this one thing about Jay, Nina's deceased husband: he is not cheap. Those quarters can add up!

Animals

Animals are another very common sign.

- Butterflies
- Ladybugs
- Dragonflies
- Birds

Birds

Birds, especially cardinals, are a well-known common sign. People believe that when a bird like a cardinal shows up on the windowsill that it's a sign from their loved ones. I've witnessed this myself.

Winter Cardinal

I had a client whose son had passed and when he's around she would see a cardinal. I did a reading for her and her son came through and mentioned that is that one of the ways he lets her know he is still in their lives.

One afternoon I was sitting at my desk looking out of the window on a cold snowy February, and there out of the blue a beautiful red cardinal flew up to my window and sat on the sill. Now with all the snow around, it was quite striking. Less than 30 seconds later my phone rang and when I answered it I recognized the voice immediately as the woman who had lost her son. She was calling me to set up an appointment to get some information about Medicare for one of her friends. I told her that right at this moment I was looking out the window at this beautiful cardinal. She started to cry and said that's my baby. That was the first time I had talked to this woman in two years!

That's a great example of sending a sign to another to have passed along. I hadn't talked to this lady in two years and she called at the exact time that this beautiful cardinal showed up my windowsill. That is the sign she receives when her son is around. It was just a perfect reminder to me how beautiful these connections can be. By the way I'd never seen a cardinal land on my sill, and it's never happened again.

And there are many, many others, but I just wanted to go over some of the most common ones.

Why do they come to us?

- To say they're OK

- To say "they made it"

- To say they still exist, still love us and will be with us throughout our life

- To show support at an appropriate time in relation to the current situations that are happening in our lives

Many times we ask if a loved one is OK, where they are, if they still remember us. So these are the reasons they like to send a sign to let us know that they're still around.

Can I ask for sign, and increase my chances of getting one?

- Yes, by asking for a sign you are giving them an invitation to make contact.

- You can do this through a simple prayer or just thinking of them will open up communications.

- Be open to the possibility.

- Believe. Be willing to accept the sign that you receive. Remember to say thank you, it lets them know you have truly accepted the sign and will increase your chances of getting more signs.

Some people are just naturals at receiving and understanding signs. They overwhelmingly believe that they happen and are truly thankful for them.

We all have a tendency to question ourselves, asking whether this was actually a sign from a deceased loved one. So we asked for another one, and then another one and then maybe one more. I've done this myself, and I should know better. So once you receive and recognize this contact, take it as a sacred event between you and your loved one. And think about the bigger picture of our lives, that life continues and love transcends death.

When you ask, ask with NO expectations. Don't put conditions on it like how you want the sign, when you want it or where.

I want a sign, just not now.

I once had a lady who wanted to ask for sign but she told me that they shouldn't send it the following week because she was going to be on vacation. And to try not to send it in the afternoon because she was at her daughter's soccer practice. Like they didn't know her schedule!

Now I bet they were rolling their eyes on the other side thinking that this woman just doesn't get it. So when you ask for the sign, let it go, and let them do the hard work.

Why not a sign?

- The person might not be ready, emotionally or mentally for contact

- Their culture or religion may hold them back from accepting a sign

- Their doubt is so strong that they would not be capable of accepting a sign

They could say "I'm open to it" but somewhere there is a block. This might be occurring subconsciously, causing a sign not to be recognized or even sent.

How do we know if it's authentic?

- A real sign will cause a real emotional response: a WOW moment; the kind that gives you goose bumps.

- A vivid dream that last many years, one that you can still remember the details like it was last night.

- You're thinking of your deceased loved one and then all of a sudden bang, there's a sign

- Once they come through they might repeat contact at the same time, place, and use the same sign. Examples of this are finding coins, repeated smells associated with your loved one or perhaps sequential numbers showing up at a particular time every night or early morning.

So hopefully you have learned a little more about signs. It's important to remind others that what is happening to them is happening to many, many other people. Just knowing that can bring peace into someone's life.

If anyone gets a sign this weekend, I'd love to hear about it!

Biography

Joe Higgins is an Amazon bestselling author and Intuitive Medium and has had the ability to communicate with those who have passed on since an early age. Joe has completed and taught classes in mediumship and advanced mediumship as well as becoming a Certified Reiki Master. He has completed the Morris Pratt Institute training and a residential course in Pastoral Skills in Lily Dale, NY. He has published three books; *Hello...Anyone Home? A Guide on How our Deceased Loved Ones Try to Contact Us through the Use of Signs, The Everything Guide to Evidence of the Afterlife: A scientific approach to proving the existence of life after death (Everything Series)* and *Always Connected for Veterans: Deceased Vets Give Guidance From The Other Side.*

Mr. Higgins's fourth book, *I Got Your Message! Understanding Signs From Deceased Loved Ones* will be available in July 2014. Mr. Higgins has become a leading authority on the process of Signs.

Hereafter Now: Connect With Loved Ones in Spirit

Susanne Wilson

Abstract

This paper contains an explanation of Susan Wilson's background as a medium. It explains that people can communicate with loved ones on the other side of the veil, and that the loved ones are anxious to make the connection as well. The paper ends with the Hereafter Now Meditation, intended for people to use to connect with their loved ones in spirit.

Hereafter Now: Connect With Loved Ones in Spirit

By Susanne Wilson

My name is Susanne Wilson. I am known as the Carefree Medium mainly because I live and work in Carefree, Arizona. I believe that no matter what happens, any of us have the potential to feel carefree. This is because the peace that surpasses understanding is always available, when we make inner peace our priority.

I am often asked "When did you first know that you are a medium?" I knew I was different as soon as I started school at age five in the Head Start program. Head Start is a federally funded program to help promote school readiness for low income children. My five-year-old self was terrified during those first weeks at school. I saw spirit lights, colors and faces around the teacher and my classmates. One day before school started, I hid in the back of the classroom behind a big rocking chair toy that was turned upside down and leaned against the back wall. The

171

teacher marked me as being absent that day, until I emerged from my hiding place at snack time. I must have been hungry.

My grandfather was a Protestant minister and mediumistic himself. He often talked with me in a comforting way about spirit. Eventually I stopped being afraid. I learned it was better to hide my abilities. When I was 14 years old, my grandfather's spirit visited me immediately after he passed. No one in our home had yet been notified of his passing. It was late and I was in bed. My grandfather awakened me. Smiling, he held out his hands and we danced elegantly as we had many times. He explained that God had called him home. He told me, "You are going to be all right." Then he disappeared and I cried. A moment later I heard the phone in the kitchen ring several times, followed by my mother answering it and then sobbing. She had just been told on the phone that her father (my grandfather) had passed unexpectedly at age 56.

As an adult I spent many years focused on living a so-called normal life. I built a successful career and made a good living. I earned my bachelor's and master's degrees from traditional universities, found my life partner, Carl whom I married in 1987. From the early 1990s, I was secretly studying psychic development and doing mini readings for friends and acquaintances.

I often say that mediumship is a calling, not a choice. I did not choose to work as a professional medium. In 2007 the universe gave me a wake-up call that literally took my breath away. I had an allergic reaction known as anaphylaxis. I was surrounded by white light. I heard beautiful spirit music that washed waves of peace through me. I felt the arms of my grandfather enfolding me. I heard a voice say that I had to go back and start my work. My near-death experience was the one minute that changed my life. I found my calling.

I provide readings and teach Reiki and intuition development classes and private lessons. Clients always want to meet their spirit guides during an intuition lesson, and thus I developed and fine-tuned a meditation designed for meeting your spirit guide.

While conducting these meditations, to my surprise, I found that more than guides were showing up for my clients. They were also connecting with their loved ones in the afterlife. The first few times this happened during my guided meditation, I thought it was because loved ones can sometimes act as helper guides. They show up in our lives at just the right time. But it started happening over and over until finally I realized: Spirit wants me to teach people how to make their own direct connection with the afterlife. Today I teach visualizations and methods to "make a date" to connect with your loved one in the afterlife. I feel that all people have the potential to make this direct connection. We can learn to dialogue through signs, symbols, synchronicities, dreams, and meditations. It is a unique and wondrous syntax, the love language of the afterlife.

I believe that the so called veil between the physical and mental planes is a quantum physical manifestation of our all-too-human belief that we are somehow separate from the creator. No one grieves alone. No one we love is ever really "lost." Grief is an honorable facet of our Earthly lives. Our deceased loved ones need not grieve. They enjoy touching base, being with us during our challenges and successes here on Earth.

Connecting with people and pets who have passed helps assuage our pain from the temporary separation. Our loved ones in the afterlife are thrilled when we acknowledge the signs they send us. They delight in the opportunity to communicate through an evidential mediumship reading from someone like me. Evidential mediumship can help heal grief, yet its primary intention is to validate that consciousness survives physical death. Ultimately you empower yourself to heal through learning and applying methods such as those presented at this conference. When you receive direct communication from your loved one in spirit, do not wonder if it is real or your imagination. Let it be. Trust the information you receive so long as it feels loving, logical, and aligned with your loved one's personality.

As a spiritual being, you have the ability to learn the love language of the afterlife. Be patient with yourself and trust. I invite you to take the next step, by using the following script from my meditation, *Hereafter Now*. This meditation, along with additional meditations, podcasts, and resources are available through my website: CarefreeMedium.com.

Please note: Conference attendees were offered the opportunity to sign-up to receive a free download of the meditation, *Hereafter Now,* and a subscription to my email newsletter. If you missed this opportunity, please contact me directly: Susanne@CarefreeMedium.com.

Hereafter Now Meditation©

by Susanne Wilson

Begin by choosing the position of your body. It is best to keep your spine straight. Yoga students may prefer the half lotus position. You may sit upright, in a chair, both feet on the floor. Or you may choose to lie down, with a pillow under your knees to support your back. Let your hands rest in your lap or at your sides with your palms facing up. Close your eyes and mouth, breathe slowly through your nose. As you inhale, visualize a white light entering your body. As you exhale, slowly let your breath all the way out. Breathing in, white light. Breathing out, stress, anxiety, your to-do list. Let go. Release. Go to zero, to center, to this moment.

Before we begin, let's affirm our words of grounding and protection:

> Divine source, holy creator, thank you for blessing me with this day, with my life and all my blessings. I am grateful for each day, each opportunity to be of service in this life and in this body. I ask you to surround me in a beautiful, translucent golden bubble of protection that is bathed in your divine white light. Sealing in all my positive energies and good health. Sealing out all negative energies and ill health, all entities from lower realms, and we send white light to the lower realms. So that only peace, love and protection may enter in. I give gratitude for my spiritual team, spirit guides, angels and all my loved ones in the light. I am grateful for their love and support as I walk the path of my life. And so it is.

Still aware of your body, let your shoulders drop and relax, your back releasing now. Visualize a golden cord appearing below you. This golden cord extends down, going deeply into mother Earth, grounding you, perfectly.

Now, visualize a beam of white light shining down from the sky, shining through the ceiling. Let this light shine upon you, entering your body thru the top of your head. The light illuminates your entire body, from your head all the way down to the soles of your feet. Brilliant, healing, divine white light.

In this divine light, all energy stuck to you that does not belong retreats now, sliding down through the golden cord beneath your seat, and down through the floor, going deeply into Mother Earth to be neutralized.

Now, think of a loved one in spirit. Invite your loved one to join you in this meditation. Send them loving thoughts. Bring forth a happy memory.

Now rest a moment while the light heals you, recharging your spiritual batteries.

Next visualize you are standing in front of a large white house. The front door to this house is open. See yourself walking forward, towards this beautiful house and through the doorway. Notice you are standing in front of a long hallway. Look down the hallway, there is an elevator at the end of the hall. Slowly begin walking towards the elevator, and notice there are rooms to your left side, and rooms to your right side. Continue walking down the hallway, and as you pass the rooms on both sides of you, each room has a bright light shining through its doorway. A different color light radiates from each room, on your left and on your right. Beautiful, laser-like colors. Red, orange, yellow, green, blue, indigo, violet. These are healing rooms. As you walk by them, you can feel the healing energy running through you. Feeling very relaxed and peaceful.

Now coming to the end of the hallway, the elevator doors are opening before you. Walk into the elevator, turn around, and the elevator doors slowly close. The elevator begins to gently rise, slowly and smoothly ascending. As the elevator rises, feel your vibration becoming higher and higher. The elevator quietly stops and the doors are opening. Exit the elevator and find yourself in a beautiful room with beautiful furniture.

You can choose the colors, the textures, fabrics, everything in this room. This is your room. Your sanctuary. Your place to relax, recharge, heal.

Notice in the middle of your room, a beautiful, pillowy chair. Go ahead, have a seat in the chair. Feel yourself sinking in, becoming even more relaxed and peaceful. Notice beside you is a small table with a remote control device. Pick up the remote control. Press the button, and notice curtains are slowly opening directly across from you. These curtains reveal a movie screen. A clear, pure white, pristine, movie screen. Put the remote control down on the table beside you, and look at the screen.

In the center of the screen, a small blue dot is appearing. The blue dot is spinning slowly, and becoming larger and larger. The light now fills the movie screen, and begins morphing, changing. Now a large wooden door fills the screen. On this door, appears a round, golden handle. This is the doorway between dimensions. The threshold to the world of spirit.

Rise up from your chair, and walk slowly towards the wooden door. On the count of three, you will pass through the door, over the threshold. Three, almost there. Two, reaching out for the golden door handle, holding the handle and pulling it towards you, opening the door. One, cross over the threshold.

Now you are standing in a forest. A lush, green forest with tall trees around you. Feel the gentle warmth of sunshine on your face. Glance down at your bare feet and feel soft, cool grass beneath them. Wildflowers of every color in the rainbow are in full bloom around you. Fresh air, luscious scents of flowers, pine, purity. There is a waterfall off in the distance, you can hear the sound of water splashing onto rocks. Deer walking through the forest, hear the crunch of leaves beneath their feet. All your senses are fully alive, vibrant. As you see. Hear. Feel.

Continue your walk in this beautiful forest, and enter a clearing. Now you are standing in front of a small building made entirely of clear, quartz crystal. Walk through the open doorway of this crystal building. As you enter, immediately feel the peaceful vibration here.

The building is brilliantly illuminated. There is no limitation to the light entering into this crystal building as it has no ceiling. Floating above you are smiling angels, wings of light. You may see a color, or colors, you may see the faces of your angels. Don't wonder if it is real, or your imagination. Simply let it be.

Your angels are showering you in divine white light. Supercharging your energy with compassion for yourself. Compassion for others. Bathing you in peace. Joy. Trust. Trust that there is a plan. Trust the divine within you. Trust that no one we love is ever really "lost."

You stand strong in this light. Connected with divine consciousness. Absorbing the light into every cell and every atom of your body. So that everyone you meet, can see their divinity in your eyes. Hear compassion in your voice. Feel healing energy from your heart.

One of the angels draws near to you. Your guardian angel, who tells you "Remember to call upon us, your angels, visit this place whenever you wish. We love you. Always."

The angels retreat now, floating softly away, but never far from you. Turn now, leaving the crystal building, back into the forest.

In front of you, a hummingbird has paused, suspended in the air near your face. See every detail of the hummingbird, hear the flutter of tiny wings. The hummingbird floats downward in front of you, showing you the pathway on which you are standing. Begin walking on the pathway, slowly. As you walk, take in the beauty of this sacred space. Feeling even more relaxed. Peaceful. Free. Continue walking.

Now, at the end of the path, notice there is a lake. A crystal clear, blue body of water. Continue walking towards the lake in this beautiful, relaxing place. Go to the water's edge, and look down into the lake. The water is pure. Clear. You can see your reflection. See yourself smiling in this reflection. Healthy. Peaceful. Free. Now, you notice there is someone joining you. Your loved one has arrived. Standing directly at your side, looking into the lake. Both of you are smiling. Notice your loved one's reflection in the lake. Happy, healthy and whole. And now, turn, face each other and embrace. See, hear and feel this happy reunion. Don't wonder if it is real or your imagination, simply let it be.

Notice, off to the side, there is a blanket and picnic basket under an enormously tall tree. A tree living here since the beginning of time. The tree of life. Have a seat together on this blanket. Enjoy each other's presence, sitting side by side.

In this sacred place, you are learning to speak a new language. It is the love language of the afterlife. A wondrous syntax of signs, symbols, emotions. Existing on the mental plane. This place *is* reality. Here. Now. Your loved one thanks you, and hugs you again.

The picnic basket beside you is filled with happy memories that you and your loved one share. Places, events, special moments. As you open the picnic basket, so many happy memories fill your heart with joy. Take a moment, and choose a happy memory of a place that you and your loved one enjoy. You will go to this place, together, in a moment. Perhaps you will choose your backyard, or the beach, a mountain, hiking trail, your boat or living room. Any place you both enjoy. Now visualize that place. See it. Hear it. Smell it. Feel it.

On the count of three you and your loved one will go together to that place. Three, reach your hand out to your loved one beside you. Two, hold hands. One, you are both there, together, completely in the moment. Nothing else exists now.

If you like, you may ask your loved one a question. Or say whatever you wish to say to your loved one. Or simply enjoy each other's company.

Remember that love lives forever. And relationships never end. You are making a new memory, now, here, in this moment, with your loved one. Being together. So much joy.

Now, you and your loved one stand up. It is time to walk back on the pathway, back in the direction from which you came. Look now at the end of the pathway, the large wooden door with the golden handle is gently opening. You are almost at the door, the threshold back to your room. Turn and face your loved one. Your loved one is happy. Perfect. Doing great, and loves you. Always.

Your loved one watches, smiling, as you approach the open doorway. On the count of three, you will walk through the doorway, and find yourself back in your room. Three, halfway there. Two, right at the threshold. One, crossing the threshold back into your room. Pick up the remote control from the table, and press the button. As you do, notice that the large wooden door on your movie screen is closing. It's becoming smaller and smaller, fading from view, as the curtains close on the screen. Now, put the remote control down. Walk back to the elevator just as the elevator doors have opened.

Enter the elevator, turn around, and see the doors gently closing as the elevator now descends, going down slowly. The elevator comes to a stop and the doors have now opened. Exit the elevator and start walking down the long hallway towards the front door of the house. This time, as you are walking down the hallway, those beautiful lights coming from the healing rooms on your left and right have intensified. As you walk by the healing rooms, the lights are supercharging your energy, your aura. Increasing your intuitive abilities. Raising your vibration, so that you are better able to recognize, the signs, symbols, and synchronicities that your loved ones in spirit are sending you, all the time. Perfect harmony of body. Mind. Soul.

The creator's house has many healing rooms. You can return here and visit anytime. You can sit or lie down in a healing room. Relax, recharge, and heal whenever you wish.

Now walking to the end of the hallway, the front door is all the way open. Walk through the front door, exiting the large white house. Now, begin walking away. Slowly walking away, and back to your physical body. With your eyes still closed, becoming more aware of your body now. It is time to call your energy back to your body.

In your mind, say "I call my energy back." Become more aware now of the chair in which you sit, feeling the seat and the back of the chair. Breathing through your nose, take a slow breath in, and a slow breath out.

You are completely back in your body now. Very relaxed, yet energized. Healthy. Whole. Peaceful.

Know and trust that you can meet with your loved ones at any time you choose. The creator has gifted you with angels to support you. Your angels are on standby. All you need do is ask for their help. Send out thoughts, prayers, gratitude and in your mind, simply prepare the place where you will meet with your loved one. See it. Hear it. Smell it. Feel your special, sacred meeting place. and choose the date and the time to invite your loved one.

Take a slow breath in, and a slow breath out. Remember, the peace that surpasses understanding is always available to you.

When you are ready, open your eyes.

You are a child of God. You are never alone. Love lives forever. And so it is. - Susanne Wilson

Biography

Susanne Wilson has a BA in management with an HR concentration, MA in public administration, and certification as a senior professional in human resources (SPHR). She has been a manager of compensation and benefits in a company, vice president of a company, founder and administrative director of the Center for Leadership and Innovation at Florida Gulf Coast University, analyst in the small business development center, and administrative manager of the Stanford University Medical Center. She is a member of the International Association of Reiki Professionals and is a Usui Reiki Master Teacher.

The Threshold Room

A sacred place to meet God and have direct
contact with loved ones who have died.

Herb Puryear, Ph.D.
Anne Puryear, D.D.

Abstract

*At The Logos Center in Scottsdale, Arizona, founded by
Anne & Herb Puryear, was a fully dedicated room called The
Threshold. It was inspired by two influences—one was the
desire for a sacred room fully designated for meditation. The
second inspiration was the Raymond Moody, MD book
<u>Reunions</u> (1994), in which he describes his "psychomanteum."*

*The room called The Threshold, as a meeting point between
dimensions, was a Faraday cage fully lined with copper
screening, containing a copper pyramid, a mirror, an amethyst
grid, Hemi-Sync CDs and other consciousness enhancing
features. The major use of this room over a 12-year period was
research on Spirit Plane communication. Three research
projects were conducted with participants who had prepared
themselves in advance with an extensive reading list and who
committed to meditating in the room several hours weekly over
an eight-week period. Of 75 participants 72% reported
experiencing a definite contact with a loved one in the Spirit
Plane. The room was also effectively used for psychic readings,
personal meditations and as the sacred place for a unique
healing team whose clients reported miraculous results.*

*Suggestions are made for how anyone may use some of the
features of this design to build their own Threshold or sacred
space. Photographs of the Threshold Room, individual energies
photographed there and around individuals will be shown in the
short Power Point presentation during our talk.*

The Threshold Room

by Anne and Herb Puryear

The Threshold Room - 10x10 foot, copper lined Faraday cage research & Meditation Room - The Logos Center, Scottsdale, Arizona

We co-founded The Logos Center in 1983 in Phoenix, Arizona, based on the teachings of Jesus, Edgar Cayce, and other spiritual leaders.

We listed The Logos Center as a meditation center, focusing our activities, programs and courses on meditation. Almost everyone who meditates desires a dedicated place for meditation, especially a dedicated room for meditation. We at The Logos Center were also deeply interested in communication with those in the Spirit Plane. Early on in her professional work in spirituality, Anne began researching Spirit Plane communication through paranormal voice recording (now called EVP). By leaving a tape running on record for a period of time, then playing it back, distinctive voices and messages could be detected, after questions were asked silently or aloud. The results of her research were published in a book and other publications.

During this time period, Anne's son Stephen, 15, passed into the Spirit Plane. Anne says: After his passing, I began to talk frequently to him, and he answered me back. He dictated the book *Stephen Lives! My Son Stephen, His Life, Suicide and Afterlife* (1997) to me. So I had a high level of confidence in communicating with him. But I had not seen him since his passing. I wanted to see Stephen.

One day, I read Dr. Raymond Moody's *Reunions: Visionary Encounters with Departed Loved Ones* (1994). Dr. Moody explained that people are able to see a loved one who has passed away by gazing into a mirror. After reading the book, I decided on a whim to give it a try. Highly doubtful that it would work, I placed a small rectangular makeup mirror on the top shelf of one of my bookcases in my office, closed the blinds and door, turned off the lights, and sat in my chair looking into the mirror, waiting to see what would happen. I kind of half prayed and half meditated while I asked Stephen to appear if he could. Nothing happened.

A half hour passed and I could not even hear Stephen, which I usually could. I started to turn on the lights and chalk the experience up as a failure, but decided since I had worked at it this long, to give it a few more minutes. I sat back down and continued gazing upward at the mirror. In a short time, a purple light appeared in the mirror and grew bigger. Then it moved out of the mirror to the right side. I blinked my eyes but the purple light stayed. I kept looking at the light. Stephen's face appeared. His face turned to the right making a side view, but it wasn't like a photograph. It was moving like when he was alive. I think I gasped, and tears filled my eyes. The vision in the mirror lasted only a minute or so but I said out loud, "There is something to this. I saw Stephen like when he was alive!"

I rushed into the bedroom and told Herb what happened. We began to discuss how to set up a room to help people communicate with loved ones who had died. We discussed Faraday cages, pyramids, mirrors, stones, gems, music and various designs. Those discussions evolved into The Threshold Project. Herb designed the room and oversaw each segment that was built.

The Design of the Threshold Room

We knew that a room shielded from extraneous sounds and electromagnetism could enhance psychic activity. This type of shielded room is called a Faraday cage. In the late fifties, Dr. Andrea Puharich and psychic Peter Hurkos demonstrated that a Faraday cage could increase psychic accuracy significantly. Sometimes Hurkos could correctly identify information not known to him using his psychic ability with 100% accuracy while sitting in the Faraday cage.

So we built a Faraday Cage in the Logos Center. It was a 10' X 10' fully dedicated meditation room. The room was completely lined with copper screening, walls, floor and ceiling, and deeply grounded with a copper rod. The metal door was also grounded. The walls, ceiling and door were doubly insulated to be as soundproof as possible.

We also surmised from published research, that a pyramid made of copper could enhance psychic ability. During the 1970s, a great deal of research was conducted demonstrating the effects of different spaces on psychic performance, such as the shape of an egg, a pyramid, and others. These various 3-D spaces were called "psychotronic generators." The theory is that there is a "life force, a "bio-energy" which some call "psychotronic energy." The pyramid, especially in the dimensional ratios found in the Pyramid of Giza, is said to be of special power in gathering these energies. This research led to the expression, "pyramid power," because it was apparent that the pyramid shape enhanced abilities. As a result, inside The Threshold Room was a copper pyramid, 10' X 10', at the base with proportions of those of the great pyramid of Giza.

Surrounding the pyramid was an amethyst grid. Dr. Richard Gerber, author of *Vibrational Medicine* (2001) gave us the instructions on how to establish a powerful energy pattern by placing an amethyst at each corner and at the apex of the pyramid.

We prepared the inside of the room to enhance psychic abilities and afterlife communication. Bill Roberts, highly respected Monroe Institute facilitator, provided us with appropriate Hemi-Sync® CD's, for our Bose player, designed to enhance higher states of consciousness.

Using what we had learned about mirror gazing from Dr. Moody's *Reunions* (1994), regarding the use of a speculum to enhance altered states of consciousness, we mounted a mirror high on the wall so that the experiencers could see into the mirror but not see themselves. With the power brought to this room by the sincere seeking and meditations of the subjects, this room became truly a sacred space.

Studies of The Threshold Room's Effects

We asked for 25 volunteers, including believers and non-believers, to participate in very intensive six-week research projects in three research programs that were held two years apart to see if The Threshold Room would enhance their ability to connect with a loved one who had died. We always had far more than 25 people who wanted to participate each time we performed this study. In each of the three programs there were slightly more women than men. Their ages varied from late 20s to 70s.

The participants were given a required-reading list before they were accepted in the program so they would better understand experiences they might have. These books were *Hello from Heaven* (1997) (Bill Guggenheim's research with over 3,000 people who had various experiences with loved ones who died), *Reunions* (1994) (Raymond Moody's wonderful, informative book), *Story of Edgar Cayce: There is a River* (1997) (the story of Edgar Cayce's journey and psychic gifts), *Stephen Lives!* (1994), *Journeys Out of the Body* (1992) ((Robert Monroe's amazing book of out-of-body experiences), *Opening Doors Within* (2007) (Eileen Caddy's book of her messages from God or that still small voice within), *Conversations with God* (1996) (Neale Donald Walsh's first book on his talks with God), and *The Edgar Cayce Primer* (1985) (Herb's best-selling book with specific chapters about what Edgar Cayce received in his trance readings).

Each of the 25 participants in the three programs filled out an extensive form of 33 questions about their backgrounds, fields of study, and books that had the most impact on their lives. They were required to write a one-page review of each of the required-reading books and were given a sheet of 20 required preparation activities for the six-week research program that they were to study and complete. They were required to commit two hours a week, for a total of 12 hours and had to agree that they had a sincere desire to attune to someone in the spirit plane and a willingness to experiment, persevere, and be open to experiences. We asked them to refrain from taking any stimulants (coffee, tea, alcohol, chocolate, colas, and sugars) for four to eight hours or more before each session, because stimulants can make it more difficult to attune.

The instructions included ways in which to prepare for better attunement, including meditation, prayer, breathing exercises, relaxation techniques, setting the intent of expecting to have an experience with a loved one who died, and taking into the Threshold a photo, piece of jewelry, or something else that belonged to the person who died.

They filled out a lengthy, detailed form before each of the 12 sessions with questions about their state of mind: whether they were anxious, nervous, and so on. When they were in The Threshold Room, participants were allowed to have a light that could be dimmed, or they could attune and meditate completely in the dark. They were given the choice of two Hemi-Sync® CDs to have playing while in the room or no music, and whether they wanted headphones or not.

A facilitator was always available to let them know when their session was over, but they were asked not to speak to the facilitator or anyone else until they filled out another lengthy form about their experiences and emotional states after the session. They had to list what music they played, what objects they brought into the room, including any stones and gems, and their choice between two aroma therapy oils available to enhance meditation.

In the Threshold Room a green chair that reclined almost completely flat was under the pyramid, facing east. The person could recline or sit up.

If they chose to meditate in the dark, their eyes would soon light adapt and they could look up and see the mirror placed high up on the wall. The edges of the mirror were covered with black velvet to make gazing into it easier and less distracting. According to our friend Richard Gerber, M.D., author of *Vibrational Medicine* (2001), who instructed us in a specific and complicated way to set an amethyst grid, we would take fifteen minutes before each week's sessions to set the grid and re-set it each following week. There were very large amethyst geodes in each corner, actually shaped like angel wings, and a small amethyst point at the apex of the pyramid. Behind the chair was a very large double terminated quartz crystal, which helps in out of body travel, according to many stone and gem experts.

Anne and I and several others at The Logos Center are Pranic Healing graduates, so after each participant finished, the room, chair and stones were sprayed with Pranic Healing spray (see Master Stephen Co's book, *Your Hands Can Heal You,* 2004, www.pranichealing.com for instructions on how to make and use the spray) to clean out any energies from the previous participant and have an energetically clean room for the next person.

Participant Experiences

Sometime between a few seconds and 20 or 30 minutes in the chair making their personal attunements and asking to communicate with someone in Spirit, the following experiences happened:

Parents had actual physical experiences with their children who had died, being touched by them and talking with them. Some could hear them speak aloud; some could hear them inside their head as if they moved their thoughts aside and spoke. Several felt their presence and saw movement in the mirror—faces and colors. One woman felt her son's hands touch hers and move them together in a dance movement they did when he was alive. Her experience lasted over 20 minutes.

Many dog lovers saw their elderly dogs that had died years before, romping in fields like they did as puppies, completely healed and well. A man trying to contact his father who died smelled the aroma of the cigarettes he used to smoke and felt his presence. Many men and women heard and saw loved ones who had died, appearing as they were in the prime of life. Frequently people asked for a message for themselves or another family member, and were amazed at what they heard, such as advice about health, relationships, and how they needed to do specific things in their lives or for a loved one. Others trying to contact a specific loved one, instead were visited in the room by another family member or friend who had died. In all of the programs, 100% of the subjects saw a rainbow of colors and movement while looking into the mirror. Almost as many saw past lives like watching a movie of how they lived and died in times past, where they recognized friends and relatives.

Results of the Three Research Programs

When results were tabulated and combined for the three research programs, 72 percent of the 75 participants had had an encounter with a loved one who died. These encounters were in five categories of experiences: actual touch, hearing a voice, feeling their presence, seeing a loved one in the room or in the mirror, and smells associated with a loved one. There were a dozen other categories, such as seeing an animal who had died, learning about past lives, and getting intuitive guidance, which over 72 percent also experienced.

It took many volunteers and staff hours of work to facilitate these projects and it is not an easy job to do. Hearing people's experiences and seeing their faces after having an encounter they had so hoped and prayed might happen, but were unable to experience before is priceless, as they say. Almost 95 percent said they were helped by the experiences and felt more relaxed and confident about contacting someone who had died.

In other uses of The Threshold Room, Herb conducted many of Anne's Life Readings, where she works in a trance state similar to the way in which Edgar Cayce worked, during that period in which she was doing personal readings, and Work Readings for the Logos work. Many of us also enjoyed this special room for our personal meditations and the Logos healing team used it for individual and group healings. Several people spent the night in The Threshold Room with reports of extraordinary dreams and experiences.

Sumer Bacon, a well-known trance medium in Arizona did a presentation at Logos in 2007 and we spent time with her in The Threshold Room afterward. Her photographer wanted to see if there were energies in the room that he could capture on film. His digital photographs showed energies they had never seen or experienced anywhere before, nor had we. An example is on the next page.

Ann Puryear, Summer Bacon meditation room, The Logos Center, AZ.   Sunday, July 29, 2007

One of the most fun experiences we had was after our Logos 2012 International Conference on After Death Communication held in Phoenix (See link on the Logos website www.logoscenter.org under "resources"). Fourteen of the speakers and conferees gathered in The Threshold Room, laughing and chanting and delighting in the high energies from the conference. Several of us remained outside for lack of room and we closed the Threshold door as they meditated and tuned in.

Some of the speakers and attendees who gathered in the room were actress and author Diane Ladd and her husband, author Robert Hunter, Jed Gaines of Oahu, Hawaii, who founded Read Aloud America that promotes literacy and encourages a love of reading to increase children's prospects for success in school and life, and whose son had died at 16, Eben Alexander, MD, neurosurgeon who had a medically verified near death experience, and became the international bestselling author of *Proof of Heaven* (2012), Jack Turner MD, of Hilo, Hawaii, neurosurgeon and author *Medicine, Miracles & Manifestations* (2009); Bill Guggenheim, best-selling author of *Hello from Heaven* (1997); Jane Katra, co-author of *Miracles of Mind* (1999) and *The Heart of the Mind* (1999); Peter Ortiz MD, and his wife Joyce Myers; Glenda Pearson, grief counselor and author of *But Should the Angels Call for Him* (2008); and Herb Puryear.

When we opened the door after half an hour, people were channeling and getting messages for each other and almost unaware that we had even interrupted them. Anne photographed orbs in the room and around individuals. (For information about orbs, see Virginia Hummel's website www.orbwhisperer.com or Sherry Anshara's website: www.orblistener.com.)

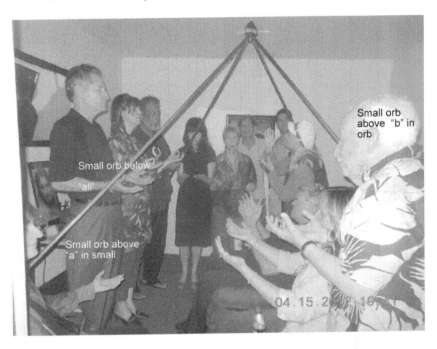

Several stayed over after the conference to use the room again and we photographed many orbs around them, and they shared their amazing experiences with us. Orbs appeared around Eben Alexander after his sessions in the room, and with his work with the healing team written about below.

A Healing Team with Amazing Results

Some of the most amazing experiences in The Threshold Room were its use by a healing team of two women who were guided by God to do a specific type of treatment. Sheri Getten, a certified healer, directed energies of healing to the client or patient, while Debra Martin, a certified Windbridge psychic medium, attuned to the person and received spiritual guidance directly from God. The reports from these patients and clients indicated miraculous healings, including restoring a young man in a coma to full healing and awareness, and Elizabeth Veney

Boisson's (founder of Helping Parents Heal
www.helpingparentsheal.com) father, a retired medical doctor and
professor whose cancer of the brain had metastasized throughout his
body, who received a few days after his treatment medical results that
showed that his cancer was completely gone. His testimony and others
are on their webpage www.goldenmiracles.com. They continue their
work now at another location, but believe the Threshold Room energies
enhanced their healing work, and credit it with giving them their start
and the energy and courage to begin this extraordinary work, and to
continue it.

Debra Martin, Eben Alexander, MD, and Sheri Getten under the copper
pyramid in The Threshold Room. The painting behind them is by William R.
Dennis called "The Threshold" depicting the space between two worlds.

An Experience with Orbs in the Threshold Room

A lovely woman whose son had died desperately wanted to have a
contact with him. When she learned about The Threshold Room, she
wanted to schedule sessions to connect with her son, but we had sold the
building and were getting ready to move out. When she found we were
moving, she quickly scheduled some sessions in it. After two sessions,
she had not established communication with her son and was
discouraged. Yet she came for one last session before we turned the
building over to the new owners. Before she came, I went into the room

and prayed and asked that God please let her have an experience with her son to help her contact him, because this would be the last session she could have in the room.

After an hour, she came out of the room, her eyes wild with excitement, and showed me some videos on her cell phone. She had called on her son and turned on her cell video recorder. Orbs moving at a fast speed (much, much harder to capture on film) came from where she was sitting and moved quickly up through the pyramid. You could clearly see them! It happened over and over on several videos. It was amazing and she and all of us believe her son communicated in this most unusual and evidential way. She has continued to get videos of orbs since that time.

You Can Build Your Own Threshold Room

You can build your own Threshold Room. It doesn't have to be as large as the one we used for 12 years in the Logos Center building. In fact, years ago a person made their bathroom into such a room and it worked beautifully for them. There are online instructions for building your own Faraday cage, using aluminum foil, copper screening or other insulators. There are also online instructions for building a Giza-type pyramid. While the pyramid in our room was copper tubing, it is the pyramid configuration not the materials of which it is made that gives the "pyramid power" effects. In his book, *The Pyramid: How to Build it, How to Use It* (1978), Les Brown gives full instructions and explanations for working with the pyramid.

Sounds, as well as fragrances, may be used to purify the room. We used a continuously-playing CD of Om chanting. The Hemi-Sync CDs are highly recommended and may be obtained from: http://shop.hemi-sync.com/shopcustcontact.asp. There is strong evidence that quartz and amethyst crystals enhance higher consciousness. When used, these need to be cleansed or reprogrammed regularly. Incense is a very powerful enhancer of altered consciousness, however, these must be carefully chosen by each individual. Try a very slight touch of Oil of Lavender to the center of the forehead, as recommended in the Edgar Cayce Readings.

Our Threshold, our Holy of Holies sacred place, could be entered only through our sanctuary, our Holy place. Prepare yourself, as did the priests of old, with prayers and centering, before you enter your Holy of Holies. Never seek to meditate or make a Spirit Plane contact without preparation and setting your intent. Such preparation will greatly influence the quality of your experience.

We are currently drawing up plans to add a similar version of The Threshold Room designed to be used in our home, in which to meditate daily and contact our loved ones and pets in the Spirit Plane.

The place you prepare may become very sacred to you. However, never feel that you must observe a specific time (although this is ideal) or be in a special place to make contact with the Spirit Plane. The more we observe specific times and places, the more likely we are to have spontaneous experiences at other times and places.

There are many ways to hear from those in Spirit. We have just personally found that this unusual room, this sacred space, makes moving across the threshold and back a bit easier and more evidential.

Contact

Anne Puryear or Herb Puryear
P.O. Box 12880
Scottsdale, Arizona 85267-2880
Phone: 480-483-9639
Herb: hpuryear@logoscenter.org
Anne: apuryea@logoscenter.org
Logos website: www.logoscenter.org
Facebook: The Logos Center:
https://www.facebook.com/groups/TheLogosCenter/
Facebook: Helping Pet Lovers Heal:
https://www.facebook.com/groups/1410983885808599/
(Website in memory of the Puryear's dog Beethoven & other animals who have died and their people are grieving)

Bibliography

Alexander, E. (2012). *Proof of Heaven: A Neurosurgeon's Journey into the Afterlife*. Simon & Schuster.

Brown, L. (1978). *The Pyramid: How to Build It, How to Use it.* Apex Publishing Company.

Caddy, Eileen. (2007). *Opening Doors Within: 365 Daily Meditations from Findhorn*. Findhorn Press.

Co, M.S. (2004). *Your Hands Can Heal You: Pranic Healing Energy Remedies to Boost Vitality and Speed Recovery from Common Health Problems*. Atria Books.

Gerber, R. (2001). *Vibrational Medicine: The #1 Handbook of Subtle-Energy Therapies*. Bear & Company.

Guggenheim, B. (1997). *Hello from Heaven: A New Field of Research— After-Death Communication Confirms that Life and Love Are Eternal*. Bantam.

Katra, J. (1999). *Miracles of Mind: Exploring Nonlocal Consciousness and Spiritual Healing*. New World Library.

Katra, J. and Targ, R. (1999). *The Heart of the Mind: How to Know God Without Believing Anything*. New World Library.

Monroe, R. (1992). *Journeys Out of the Body*. Broadway Books.

Moody, R. (1994). *Reunions: Visionary Encounters with Departed Loved Ones*. My books.

Pearson, G. (2008). *But Should the Angels Call for Him. A Mother's Journey Through Grief and Discovery*. Xlibris.

Puryear, A. (2000). *Messages from God*. New Paradigm Books.

Puryear, A. (1997). *Stephen Lives! My Son Stephen, His Life, Suicide and Afterlife*. Gallery Books.

Puryear, H. (1995). *Why Jesus Taught Reincarnation: A Better News Gospel*. New Paradigm Press.

Puryear, H. (1985). *The Edgar Cayce Primer: Discovering the Path to Self Transformation*. Bantam.

Sugrue, T. (1997). *Story of Edgar Cayce: There Is a River*. A.R.E. Press.

Turner, J.L. (2009). *Medicine, Miracles, and Manifestations: A Doctor's Journey Through the Worlds of Divine Intervention, Near-Death Experiences, and Universal Energy*. Career Press.

Walsch, N.D. (1996). *Conversations with God: An Uncommon Dialogue*. G. P. Putnam's Sons.

Biographies

Herb Puryear, Ph.D., is a clinical psychologist who graduated from Stanford and the University of North Carolina. He has been consultant to psychiatric hospitals, a professor of psychology at Trinity University, director of research and education at the Cayce Foundation in Virginia Beach, and president of Atlantic University. He is the author of eight books, including *The Edgar Cayce Primer* (1985), (published by Bantam) *Reflections on the Path, Sex & The Spiritual Path* (published by St. Martins), and *Why Jesus Taught Reincarnation* (1995). He was the host of two series for PBS, and lectures worldwide about his research on spiritual truths. He currently has several books in different stages ready for publication.

Anne Puryear, D.D., received her ministerial degree in Washington, D.C. She began a research center investigating paranormal experiences and teaching students to develop their ESP. A Gestalt Therapist, she was co-founder of Life Guidance Foundation, and later began giving life readings in a trance state similar to Edgar Cayce. She gave over 10,000 readings for the A.R.E. Clinic in Phoenix, Arizona, in special medical programs, and in her private practice and at The Logos Center. She conducted 16 research programs for children to help them develop their intuitive and healing abilities. Anne is the author of *Stephen Lives! My Son Stephen, His Life, Suicide & Afterlife (1997)* and *Messages from God* (2000) (currently going into its fourth publication). *Stephen Lives!* is being made into a movie and the rewrite of the screenplay is currently having additions made to it. Anne is working on three new books due out next year, including one about the legacy of Beethoven, their beloved dog who died recently.

My Experiences with Physical Medium David Thompson

Victor Zammit, Ph.D.

Abstract

I regard materializations as the greatest discovery in human history. Imagine being in a room with a small group of people and suddenly another person appears. He/she walks around the room, talks to you in his own voice, touches you and shares intimate memories. For the last seven years of my life, my wife Wendy and I have been having these experiences on a regular basis with Sydney-based materialization medium David Thompson. During that time we have been present at more than 200 sittings and witnessed more than 100 reunions of people with their materialized loved ones. We have thoroughly investigated David's mediumship and are totally convinced it is genuine. For me this is the ultimate proof of the afterlife. Because materialization is beyond the "boggle threshold" for many people, it attracts a huge amount of skepticism to the extent that physical mediumship is now virtually unknown in the United States.

My Experiences with Physical Medium David Thompson

Victor Zammit Ph.D.

This paper is about my experiences with materialization medium David Thompson. I regard materialization as the greatest discovery in human history. This is because of all the different kinds of mediumship, only in materializations do we end up with a solid bodied person from the spirit world walking around the room. He talks to everyone present and recognizes his loved ones in the room. He shares intimate memories and when conditions are right embraces loved ones. These are repeatable experiments which consistently get the same results over time and in many different countries. I state that this has to be the most sensational evidence for the existence of the afterlife.

What is physical mediumship?

Physical Mediumship is when spirits communicate in a way that anyone present can see hear or feel. It is different to the more well-known mental mediumship where an invisible spirit impresses the mind of the medium who then passes on a message to those present.

Physical mediumship is now *extremely* rare—we know of no physical mediums currently demonstrating publicly in the United States and only a handful in England and Europe. Some physical mediums produce just materialized hands that touch sitters; others produce just voices; the most highly developed produce full materialization.

What is materialization?

During a sitting, the medium, while in deep trance, exudes ectoplasm, a whitish gaseous substance, from his nose and/or mouth. A spirit uses this ectoplasm to coat his/her spiritual body and become temporarily solid. The materialized spirit then walks around the room quite independent of the medium, who remains in trance in a curtained off area that concentrates the ectoplasm.

A brief history of physical mediumship

Physical mediumship has been known throughout history; many indigenous cultures seem to have had physical mediums- sometimes called shamans (Borgas 1904; Jones-Hunt 2010, 93-187). The Bible is full of reports of physical mediumship (Findlay 1949; Jones-Hunt 2010, 231-378; Schwartz 2014).

From the middle of the nineteenth century physical mediumship became very popular in the United States and all over Europe. Some of the best physical mediums of the day were investigated at length by the top scientists, judges, and lawyers who concluded that the effects were real and there was no fraud (Tymn, 2008). Dr. Geley and Prof. Richet conducted experiments on physical mediumship in France. During one meeting, some 150 people, including scientists, witnessed materializations (Fodor, 1960, p. 131).

In the twentieth century there were some really brilliant materialization mediums—such as Helen Duncan and Alec Harris in the United Kingdom. In the 1920s, there was the highly gifted Mirabelli in Brazil. In the United States, there have been a number of excellent materialization mediums including Ethyl Post Parrish.

What is ectoplasm.

The best known way of producing materializations involves a team in the spirit world taking a substance called ectoplasm from the body of the medium and also sometimes from some sitters. They say that they use it to lower their vibrations and become solid.

Professor Richet, winner of the Noble Prize for Physiology, studied ectoplasm closely and writes about it in his book *Thirty Years of Psychical Research* (Richet 1923). Professor Albert Baron Von Schrenck-Notzing, a Munich physician, showed that ectoplasm is composed of leucocytes—white or colorless blood cells—and epithelial cells—those from the various protective tissues of the body (Schrenck-Notzing 1923). We know that it is taken from the pancreas of the medium and that the medium experiences a huge change in blood sugar levels before and after a sitting. We also know that many physical mediums develop diabetes.

One of the key properties of ectoplasm is that some of its forms are extremely sensitive to light. Even flashing a torch drives the substance back into the medium's body with the force of snapped elastic. Bruises, open wounds and hemorrhage may result. There are many examples in the history of physical mediumship where mediums were cut, bruised and severely injured by sitters trying to grab the materialized forms which then dissolved. Because of this sensitivity to light, most physical mediums have to work in the dark or in infrared light and those responsible for their safety have to use absolute care in selecting sitters who can be trusted to stay still and hold hands during materialization (see Zammit 2013, 138-140).

Recently a German medium from the Felix Circle has been regularly demonstrating the production of ectoplasm and taking digital photos.

Today, there is no doubt that ectoplasm is real and only uninformed low level skeptics repeat the claim that ectoplasm is nothing but cheesecloth.

Our investigations of David Thompson

David was born in England and became a mental medium from the age of 17. His grandmother was a working medium and his mother has the gift. About 20 years ago at the age of 30 he began to develop as a physical medium by sitting with a "development circle" in a darkened room for about two years.

Eight years ago he relocated to Sydney Australia and invited me and my wife Wendy to investigate his mediumship.

We had exceptional access to the medium. We were with him before and after weekly séances, setting up different rooms for séances and traveling with him internationally. We spent time together socially and with his family. This is a totally different experience from sitting as a guest in public séances or even coming in for a few days of investigations.

We were given full access to audiotapes of his sessions over the previous ten years and were able to interview people who had been with him from the beginning of his mediumship. During this time we were free to observe everything that happened and make any requests for controlled conditions. We placed recorders anywhere in the séance room including immediately around the person of the medium. We edited the audiotapes of séances and would certainly have been in a position to detect any fraud if it had occurred.

We were able to interview visitors who had been reunited with loved ones using our skills and professional experience in psychological assessment and legal interviewing. We also travelled to the United Kingdom to interview people who had experienced remarkable mediumship sessions and healings with David many years before.

Over seven years we have sat in more than 200 materialization sessions and witnessed more than a hundred reunions of materialized spirits with their loved ones.

We have since been able to introduce a number of other international investigators to David's mediumship, all of whom have written testimonials attesting to its genuineness. These include Ron Pearson and Dr. Fiona Bowie in England, Professor Jan. W. Vandersande, Dr. R. Craig Hogan, and Tom and Lisa Butler in the USA.

What precautions against fraud are taken in a séance?

In a typical public materialization séance, all dealings with the sitters are arranged by the host so that the medium does not see them or even know who they are in advance.

On the night of the sitting the room, and everything in it, is thoroughly searched by two volunteer checkers. Any globes are removed from the room so that the lights will not be switched on by accident.

Everyone who will be in the séance room, including the medium and the Circle leader (the person who looks after the medium while he is in trance) is searched before entering. Everyone is also "wanded" with a metal detector. This is so that people will know that any objects that are apported into the room by spirit were not smuggled in and that the medium was not carrying in any props or masks. It is also to protect the medium by ensuring that no one is carrying a torch or anything capable of producing light.

The medium is seated in a simple chair with arms, inside a curtained off enclosure. There are straps affixed to the chair to buckle in both wrists and ankles. These straps are secured tight enough to prevent the medium from withdrawing his arms. They are then secured with one way plastic cable ties which can only be cut with wire cutters. The only pair of cutters allowed in the room is held by a member of the audience. The medium has a gag placed across his mouth and tied in a knot at the back of his head which is also secured with a one-way plastic cable tie. Under these conditions, it is impossible for the medium to stand up, walk or talk.

The sitters are seated in a semicircle around the medium and instructed to hold hands with the person next to them whenever a spirit materializes. Everyone is instructed to hold hands and immediately shout out if the person next to them tries to move.

What happens during the sitting?

After that all lights are put out and the Circle leader says a short prayer for protection of the medium and the sitters.

Recorded music is then turned on. Usually it is a mixture of popular, classical and hymns with an uplifting mood. We are informed from the afterlife that the music helps to raise the vibrations in the séance room so that the spirits don't have to lower their vibrations so far. Also the music helps the medium to go into a deep trance.

During the playing of the music, ectoplasm will be taken from the medium by one of the spirits who has been trained in the procedure and very shortly afterwards we hear the familiar "whoosh" sound that signals a spirit is materializing.

William's messages

William Charles Cadwell, who died in 1897 and describes himself as David's spirit friend and mentor, is always the first to materialize. William walks around the séance room; he claps his hands and stamps his feet to show people he is solid. He shakes hands with one or two of the sitters and places his large hand on some heads people's heads after asking permission. Everyone comments that William's hand is much larger than the medium's hand. William talks to the sitters and they talk to him; he goes straight to people without fumbling in the dark and always remembers visitors even from years before. His voice has never varied in twenty years.

We ask William about the conditions in the afterlife because what he and other highly credible afterlife teachers tell us is fundamentally inconsistent with what religion tells us. I have time to deal very briefly with five critical questions:

1. What happens on crossing over?

William tells us that we are always met by someone to help us move on to the realm of the Light. William tells us the Church's theology on crossing over is not correct: there will be no St. Peter and God waiting to pronounce judgment on you.

2. Is there eternal damnation?

William tells us that this teaching is wrong. There is no eternal damnation in the afterlife. We humans are in fact part of the Divine, and cannot be eternally damned.

3. Does the Church have authority to tell us about the afterlife?

No, we were informed the church has what is called "subjective" authority. This means the Church gave itself authority it did not have— obtaining its authority from religious writings of thousands of years ago.

4. Can anyone alter the law of cause and effect?

William said that no one on Earth has the powers to change the Law of Cause and Effect. This principle also goes for the Catholic Church's claim that it has the powers to completely forgive sins and reduce time in "purgatory" in return for donations. That is certainly not correct. Catholic priests do NOT have any powers to change the Law of Cause and Effect by one iota.

5. Are we contacting devils?

Rubbish, William says. We can make contact with loved ones who crossed over recently or decades ago. They are very keen to make contact with us. This becomes clear during our reunions.

Reunions

David Thompson is one of very few mediums in the world able to bring through people from the other side to make contact with their loved ones sitting in the séance room. If the energy is right in a séance, up to three loved ones will materialize.

One of the most emotional reunions we ever witnessed was between a lady named Sarah whose partner Nick had been killed in an accident five months earlier. Listen to an extract of the recording [available on my website http://victorzammit.com/afterlifevoices/index.htm]

Nick: Listen to me, listen to me we haven't got long. Listen to me.

Sarah: OK, my baby.

Nick: Always remember....

Sarah: Yeah?

Nick: I love you with all my heart.

Sarah: OK.

Nick: I told you that just before I left you.

Sarah: I know.

Nick: I'll always be with you. I'll always be with you.

Sarah: OK my darling.

Nick: Promise me something. I want you to be happy.

Sarah: I will for you. I will for you. I'll make the best of what I've got here. For you.

Nick: Remember whatever happens we'll always be together when we meet again.

Sarah: You promise me that?

Nick: I promise you.

Sarah: You...

Nick: From the bottom of my heart, I promise you.

Sarah: OK my darling.

Nick: I want you to be…. happy.

Sarah: I will try. I am trying. I'm trying so hard. It's just such a shock you know. But I'm trying hard. I'm doing better Darling.

Nick: You are, girl, and you're doing fantastic.

Sarah: As long as I've got you with me and I know I do. I just hope I did enough for you.

Nick: Yes you did, you were everything I ever wanted.

Sarah: I was… good. I just wanted to be enough.

Nick: That's why I died peacefully.

Sarah: You…Oh, thank goodness.

Nick: That's why I had that look of peace on my face.

Sarah: Yes. Did you see me when I went to see… you?

Nick: I did. And everything you put into the coffin. I saw it all.

Sarah: Oh, thank you darling. I tried to do right by you. I tried to do everything I could. I really tried hard.

Nick: You done more than any man could ever want. More than any man could ever want.

Sarah: OK my baby because you know you were worth it. Don't ever doubt how much I loved you and how much I will continue to love you. Don't ever doubt it.

Nick: Don't ever doubt my love for you.

Sarah: OK my baby

{Nick places his hands around Sarah's face in an embrace}

Sarah: Oh!! Oh I love you. I love you. {Sounds of dematerialization}

Among many others, Wendy's father, my sister, the husband of one good friend and the father of two other good friends all materialized. The talk is always intimate, of things that no one on Earth could know except the person concerned.

The most common messages they bring are:

- I love you.
- Be happy.

- Thank you for all you did.
- Don't blame yourself.
- I'm so proud of you.
- I see things differently now.
- I'm sorry I didn't tell you I loved you.

Sometimes there are those who come through speaking in foreign languages. We've had German, Russian and even Chinese.

Spirit VIPS.

During these materializations we had some celebrities coming through. Members of David's spirit team who frequently materialize include Sir Arthur Conan Doyle, entertainer Quentin Crisp (who tells us that there is no discrimination against gay people in the afterlife) and Louis Armstrong.

[Voices from these spirit visitors can be heard at http://victorzammit.com/afterlifevoices/index.htm]

We also had visits from well-known psychical researchers Montague Keen, David Fontana, Arthur Findlay and Tom Harrison, as well as mediums Leslie Flint, Doris Stokes, Gordon Higginson and Helen Duncan.

Harry Houdini, who was in life a close friend of Sir Arthur Conan Doyle, came through on at least five occasions. I asked Houdini how he would make up for telling lies about certain genuine mediums and go about convincing the world that there really is an afterlife. He was defensive but he promised that he would do something exceptional to prove that he is who he claims to be. Some months later he again materialized and apported a coin which showed his face.

Objections over-ruled

Over the years we had skeptics raising objections about materializations. Some of the most frequent– all invalid—include:

1. that David has confederates working with him to get his results.
   This is absolute nonsense because David travels around the world on his own—he does not have a team to go with him.

2. Unless it happens in light it's not happening.

This is a low level of objection because experts in evidence all accept that just because there is darkness does not mean activity cannot happen.

3. David is doing all the talking.

That is impossible because David is unconscious and gagged with a strong gag around his mouth; he would not be able to say anything at all.

4. It's above my "boggle threshold." Of course, for the uninformed that would be understandable until one does some research.

How sure are you that these materializations are real?

Over the last twenty-five years of handling closed-minded skeptics I formulated the five levels of evidence and applied them to David Thompson's materializations.

1. The lowest level is anecdotal evidence, with a confidence value of say 5%. Wrong! I said the level of proof for David's materializations is higher.

2. The second level is the prima facie evidence test. Confidence value 30%.

WRONG AGAIN, I said. The level of proof is higher.

3. Third, it just passes the balance of probabilities test: say 55%.

WRONG AGAIN, I said. It's higher than that.

4. Fourth is the test used in a murder trial: beyond reasonable doubt. 95%. NO, I said. David's level of proof is beyond reasonable doubt.

5. Finally, the Cartesian test—after Descates: "Doubt anything that can be doubted!!" 100% sure. I am convinced that David's materializations are beyond doubt.

Handling Skeptics

Because physical mediumship is so far outside the paradigm of materialistic science, it always attracts a great deal of skepticism. So much so that every physical medium has to battle being called fraudulent. This is so pervasive in the United States that even members of the Spiritualist community are not aware that Spiritualism was founded on physical mediumship and that the Fox sisters were extensively tested by scientists and found to be genuine. Many cannot name even one American physical medium.

In the course of my years of defending genuine psychic research I have learned some strategies that may be helpful to mediums and those working in psychic research.

1. Do not invite skeptics to participate or oversee your psychic or paranormal experiments. These usually closed-minded skeptics do not have the objectivity, the skills and the ability to perceive the paranormal with true empirical equanimity.

2. Do not debate closed-minded skeptics especially if you are a medium or a psychic. This is because these skeptics are aggressive and will use the information you give them to publicly denigrate you and the paranormal.

3. Do not fall for the trap by being told you are wrong because you are not a 'critical thinker'. Every investigator of the paranormal begins as an open-minded skeptic. We only change little by little because of the evidence. We, afterlife investigators and paranormalists, do have the evidence to show we can prove all our claims. But these skeptics do not understand that they are NOT being critical thinkers themselves. Why? Because they start by assuming that there is absolutely no validity in the paranormal and then won't examine the evidence.

4. Don't let them call you a "believer." Tell them that you are not a believer but someone who accepts the evidence. And don't rely on only one aspect of the evidence to prove your argument that the afterlife exists- in our book I outline twenty different areas of afterlife evidence.

5. If they ask you why you haven't taken on the skeptics' million dollar challenge tell them that you have investigated it and it's the biggest fraud in paranormal history. There is no million dollar challenge (see Zammit 2013, 237). And then remind them that they haven't taken up Victor Zammit's challenge to disprove the existing evidence for the afterlife.

6. If someone calls you a fraud, remind them of the recent Sally Morgan case where a flamboyant medium sued a mainstream newspaper in England—the Daily Mail—and won $250,000. The critical thing is that anyone who claims fraud has to *prove* specifically what aspect of the demonstration was fraudulent and how the fraud was carried out.

7. You can tell the skeptics that whereas no genius skeptical professor, no genius materialist, no genius closed-minded skeptic ever wrote a book that there is no afterlife, there are over a hundred scientists who *after* they investigated the afterlife evidence using their scientific expertise, wrote books saying that they accepted the evidence that there is an afterlife.

8. Finally I would advise you all to become familiar with the research outside your own area of expertise. I strongly advise you to join the Academy of Spirituality and Paranormal Studies and to read its publications. I would also recommend that you purchase a copy of our book *A Lawyer Presents the Case for the Afterlife* (2013) (available from Amazon.com) and stay up to date by subscribing to our free Friday Afterlife Reports which we have been sending out for the last 14 years.

Finally always remember with confidence that we are on the winning side!

Bibliography

Bogoras, W. (1904). Iddes religiewes des Tchouktchis (Bulletins et MCmoires, Society d'Anthropologie de Paris,Vol. 5, pp. 341-54, Paris).

Findlay, A. (1939). *The Psychic Stream,* London: Psychic Press.

Fodor, N. (1934). *The Encyclopedia of Psychic Science*. London: Arthurs Press.

Jones-Hunt, J. (2010). *Moses and Jesus: The Shamans*. Airesford: O Books.

Richet, C. (1923). *Traité de Métapsychique*.1922. English ed. as *Thirty Years of Psychical Research*. New York: Macmillan.

Schrenck-Notzing, B. (1923). *The Phenomena of Materialization*. London: Keegan Paul.

Schwartz, S. (2014). *The Bible as Psychic History*. Create Space.

Tymn, M. (2008) *The Articulate Dead*. Minnesota: Galde Press.

Zammit, V. and W. (2013). *A Lawyer Presents the Evidence for the Afterlife*. Guildford: Whitecrow.

Biography

Victor James Zammit, B.A. Dip.Ed. M.A. LL.B. Ph.D, worked as an attorney in the Local Courts, District, and Supreme Courts in Sydney Australia. Through his investigations he was astonished to discover a hidden world of research that he felt provided overwhelming evidence for life after death. He has been sharing this globally in his website www.victorzammit.com and his free weekly *Afterlife Reports* for the last 14 years. He is the co-author of *A Lawyer Presents the Evidence for the Afterlife* (2013) which outlines more than 20 different areas of afterlife evidence. It is available from all online bookshops.

Made in the USA
Lexington, KY
22 September 2014